CHANG

BCS, THE CHARTERED INSTITUTE FOR IT

BCS, The Chartered Institute for IT, is committed to making IT good for society. We use the power of our network to bring about positive, tangible change. We champion the global IT profession and the interests of individuals, engaged in that profession, for the benefit of all.

Exchanging IT expertise and knowledge
The Institute fosters links between experts from industry, academia and business to promote new thinking, education and knowledge sharing.

Supporting practitioners
Through continuing professional development and a series of respected IT qualifications, the Institute seeks to promote professional practice tuned to the demands of business. It provides practical support and information services to its members and volunteer communities around the world.

Setting standards and frameworks
The Institute collaborates with government, industry and relevant bodies to establish good working practices, codes of conduct, skills frameworks and common standards. It also offers a range of consultancy services to employers to help them adopt best practice.

Become a member
Over 70,000 people including students, teachers, professionals and practitioners enjoy the benefits of BCS membership. These include access to an international community, invitations to a roster of local and national events, career development tools and a quarterly thought-leadership magazine. Visit www.bcs.org/membership to find out more.

Further information
BCS, The Chartered Institute for IT,
First Floor, Block D,
North Star House, North Star Avenue,
Swindon, SN2 1FA, United Kingdom.
T +44 (0) 1793 417 424
F +44 (0) 1793 417 444
(Monday to Friday, 09:00 to 17:00 UK time)
www.bcs.org/contact
http://shop.bcs.org/

CHANGE MANAGER

Tracey Torble

Published by BCS Learning and Development Ltd, a wholly owned subsidiary of BCS, The Chartered Institute for IT, First Floor, Block D, North Star House, North Star Avenue, Swindon, SN2 1FA, UK.
www.bcs.org

Paperback ISBN: 978-1-78017-464-8
PDF ISBN: 978-1-78017-465-5
ePUB ISBN: 978-1-78017-466-2
Kindle ISBN: 978-1-78017-467-9

Ebook available

British Cataloguing in Publication Data.
A CIP catalogue record for this book is available at the British Library.

Publisher's acknowledgements
Reviewers: Andrew Wilkes and Bob Black
Publisher: Ian Borthwick
Commissioning editor: Rebecca Youé
Production manager: Florence Leroy
Project manager: Sunrise Setting Ltd
Copy-editor: Denise Bannerman
Proofreader: Barbara Eastman
Indexer: Matthew Gale
Cover design: Alex Wright
Cover image: Terry Kettlewell
Typeset by Lapiz Digital Services, Chennai, India

CONTENTS

LIST OF FIGURES AND TABLES

AUTHOR

Tracey Torble accidentally fell into IT in the 1980s after making a case for replacing an electric typewriter with a word processor to improve the turnaround time of some job description amendments and to meet an aggressive schedule of meetings linked to organisational change. Forever after a reluctant 'expert', she eventually gave up the business side completely to invent a helpdesk out of a brick phone, a satchel of floppy disks and a screwdriver.

This led her to a proper IT job with real processes managing technical support staff at the BBC. Told by her line manager that she would be chairing the newly formed change advisory board for the West London region she began a love–hate relationship with change management that has lasted for 20 years.

A successful career as a freelance IT service management consultant and interim manager for service desks, support and, of course, change management, led her to experience a wide range of public- and private-sector organisations, large and small, with a variety of tools, some designed for the job, some spanners as hammers, until all that remained was a passion for change. Not technical change; just change.

Refreshment came in the guise of an Open University degree in Humanities, which was followed by a post-graduate certificate in Online and Distance Education to give it a semblance of work-related respectability. A passion for writing led to further training and a mission to present IT service management as relevant at all levels of IT, with a plain language approach that hopefully shares some of the common sense that everyone says best practice is, once they have seen the answers.

FOREWORD

Organisations do not stand still. Instead, they are a moving feast of activities focused around change. Some changes are larger than others and each change has its attributes and features that make it unique. Organisational change is a result of strategic, tactical and operational pressures. These pressures can start off anywhere in the organisation and they can be structured or unstructured in nature. Often described as 'key drivers', changes can be transformational in nature or just solve an immediate underlying problem. Some need fast action and some can be taken at a more leisurely pace. Changes usually focus on people doing some action to achieve a new objective. As a result of 'the people factor', tensions and resistance to change can occur. It requires firm management and leadership across the organisation to make sure organisational change is successful. Within this mix sits the technology department, whose primary role is to maintain homeostasis for the IT systems (and services) it manages. With the pressures within the organisation itself, and the important role that IT now plays in that, it is little wonder that the role of IT change manager can be a difficult job.

Today, the role of the IT change manager sits juxtaposed between the technology department and the other similar managerial roles within an organisation. With the current focus being on digital transformation there is bound to be an evolving transformative element within the change environment. This adds a further burden on organisational staff who are directly responsible for handling change issues. If something goes wrong, they are often targeted for blame. If a change endeavour is successful, they can be the fortunate recipients of praise, but more likely success is expected as that is the very tenet of the role they play. Praise, therefore, might be in short supply and blame can come in bucket-loads.

The role of a particular person who is responsible for marshalling the 'change effort' in the technology department is even more tense. The ubiquitous nature of technology within organisations means if something goes wrong with an IT change, the effects can be catastrophic. This can have a negative effect on the organisation itself and do immeasurable harm to the IT department in particular. In an ideal world, the onus on a successful technology change is about 'team effort'.

In the early days, the task was under the heading of 'change control', under the auspices of quality management systems. Within IT, it usually resided within what was then known as the database management team. This was because of the increased organisational dependency on data and information, which in turn depended upon the reliability of corporate software systems. The software had to work and, by default, the software applications team became de facto change agents. The history is important, because the attributes of an IT change agent, and what was expected of them, helped design the role of the traditional IT change manager, which became a crucial part of the IT environment.

With the advent of IT best practice, these attributes have been expanded and around it has developed a set of interrelated processes and activities we now know as IT change management. This has created a legacy in which the designers of IT change have simply added on some extra elements to what existed already, while still allowing it to fit neatly into the mindset of the science and technology discipline. In itself, this can lead to a false premise, that the most important role of an IT change manager is someone who designs a change process and then manages and reviews it; end of.

In reality, the role of IT change manager equates to that of a captain of a ship. Change managers need to have enough technical knowledge to command respect from those on the 'deck', consider legal constraints, avoid hazards and be mindful of security. Above all, they need to keep the 'change ship' steady by getting the best out of people they are working with and communicating effectively throughout the 'change voyage'. IT change is therefore a series of journeys, some small and some big. The contemporary IT change manager needs a common-sense approach to change, while at the same time being mindful of the responsibilities the role demands.

There are many books that explain the processes and activities involved in IT change. Often, they are written for a more technical audience. Well written though they are, they tend to espouse approaches to change with that in mind. Equally, there are many books written about change from an organisational perspective. To my mind, what has been missing for quite a while are texts and even general advice that explain change in the context of the organisation and the technology department combined.

Tracey's approach is unique. It, rightly, concentrates on managing IT change from a technology viewpoint, but it also explores IT change from a wider standpoint. During her career, Tracey has investigated the challenges to the role of the IT change manager within the context of the organisation. For that reason, this is an important book that has been long overdue. Therefore, it is a pleasure for me to write this Foreword at what is a crucial time for the IT industry. The narrative within this book is built upon Tracey's vast experience in the role, which she has matured progressively over the past two decades. It is constructed on practical advice, exploring many of the myths about the IT change manager but delivered with a sense of humour and, importantly, a huge dose of realism. The book unravels the mystique surrounding IT change and in particular the practical steps required for those embarking on a role in IT change management by shattering the myth that it is just all about technology.

Sandra Whittleston
IT Service Management Educator and Researcher
Open University
December 2018

ACKNOWLEDGEMENTS

Special thanks to Andy Torble, software developer (and husband), for his insights into the workings of Agile methodologies and their relationship with change management.

Thanks also to Mark Smith, currently Senior Change and Service Coordinator at The British Red Cross, and his extensive experience of technical change management, and to Jim Hill, Business and IT Consultant/Programme Manager, currently working at Whitbread PLC, for his perspective on current practice and his mantra that if you want someone to do something you must make it the easiest option, which is the key to successful process implementation.

ABBREVIATIONS AND GLOSSARY

Agile	collective term for dynamic software development approaches
BCS	BCS, The Chartered Institute for IT
BSI	British Standards Institution
CAB	change advisory board
CHMG	SFIA/SFIA*plus* code for technical change management
CI	configuration item
CMBoK	Change Management Body of Knowledge
CMI	Change Management Institute
CMS/CMDB	change management system/database
COBIT®	Control Objectives for Information and Related Technologies
CPD	continuing professional development
CPU	central processing unit
CQI	Chartered Quality Institute
CS	change schedule
DevOps	an Agile approach to software development and IT operations
IEC	International Electrotechnical Commission
ISO	International Organization for Standardization
ITIL®	Information Technology Infrastructure Library
ITSM	IT Service Management
itSMF	IT Service Management Forum

PIR	post-implementation review
PRINCE2®	PRojects IN Controlled Environments, a project management method
PRINCE2 Agile®	a variation of PRINCE2® for Agile approaches
PSO	projected service outage
QMS	quality management system
R&D	research & development
RFC	request for change
ROI	return on investment
SaaS	software-as-a-service
SACM	service asset and configuration management
Scrum	an Agile approach to software development
SFIA	Skills Framework for the Information Age
SFIA*plus*	BCS development of SFIA
SMS	service management system
WCAG	Web Content Accessibility Guidelines

PREFACE

IT change management has often had a bad name. First, it was accused of being nosy when it intervened in the technical tinkering that was traced from unplanned disruption to IT services on Monday mornings. Now it is accused of being nosy towards reformed tinkerers who indignantly say they no longer need change management.

The problem with change management is that it hasn't changed when everything else has. IT has grown up. Its methods and techniques have improved, and it has a much more responsible attitude. Change management must grow with it and cut some slack to those with maturing processes that incorporate elements of good practice without having to be told. It won't survive if it tries to hold on to everything. But, equally, it must not let the baby be thrown out with the bathwater, or we'll be right back where we started.

The good news is that the change manager is more important than ever. When one size fits all is in danger of becoming one size fits no one, the change manager is best placed to know when to stick or twist to deliver a flexible solution that meets all needs without getting in anyone's way. Like its name suggests, the role of the change manager must shape-shift and serve up the right version of change management for the prevailing and sometimes conflicting methods of service delivery. Change keeps changing. Change managers must too.

This book is part of the BCS Guides to IT Roles series and looks at the role of change manager. It aims to clarify the role and provide guidance to practitioners who may be at varying stages of evolution in the role, which can exist at different levels of maturity.

Already the title raises questions. 'Change manager' is a generic term that can be applied in any context, but the term is used across a variety of roles even in the context of IT, where a change manager can be different things to different people.

This book is not about all of them, but in writing about one it is necessary to define them all.

WHEN IS A CHANGE MANAGER NOT A CHANGE MANAGER?

There are three types of change manager that can be involved in IT.

Usually on the outside, but known to and affecting IT, might be a business change manager responsible for overall organisational change. Change in this context could relate to products or services, restructuring for efficiency, expanding for growth, or all the above and more. The context in this case is all-encompassing, from conception of a change at board level to its implementation on the front line in terms of process, tools, knowledge, skills and behaviours, including changing the mindset of people to embrace and deliver new capabilities.

Within this wide remit might be another change manager, responsible for the digital transformation part of an overarching plan that includes modernising ways of working through the implementation of new technology. This change manager might report to an actual or notional business change manager and represent the bridge between old and new ways of working – one foot in the business and one in IT.

Then there is the change manager responsible for maintaining the integrity of the technology that delivers the organisation's products or services. This change manager is at the nuts and bolts end of IT change, looking at the impact of technical change on the overall operational technical platform and making sure that changes introduced are done so with minimal risk to existing services as part of a range of IT service management processes. In this context, the changes might relate to large-scale organisational change, digital transformation projects or 'just' business-as-usual upgrades, maintenance and fixes. A standard day in the life of this change manager might touch on all three.

Although these different change manager types can co-exist, it is this IT-specific change manager that is the subject of this guide, which seeks to place this important aspect of change management as part of IT service management within the wider context for the benefit of IT practitioners. In so doing, this book aims to help those at any point on the change management continuum to integrate transformation, significant technical change and plain old churn as seamlessly as possible to ensure continuing stability of the tools that business relies on day in and day out.

SFIA*plus*

SFIA*plus*, an extension of Skills Framework for the Information Age (SFIA) developed by BCS for its members, is the most established and widely adopted IT skills, training and development model reflecting current industry needs. It provides employers and IT practitioners with the facility to map skills against frameworks to identify training and development requirements.

SFIA*plus* provides comprehensive coverage of all three types of change management and the skills involved. For further information, go to the BCS website and look at the section on Change and Transformation, for Business Change Management and Business Change Implementation skills; and the section on Delivery and Operation for Change Management (technical) skills.[1]

---

1 https://rolemodel.bcs.org/BrowseSFIAPlus/SFIAplus/Report.ashx?r=2259_1&tab=2 (members only).

Figure 0.1 links the different types of change manager to their related SFIA*plus* skills.

Figure 0.1 Change manager at different levels, but with related functions

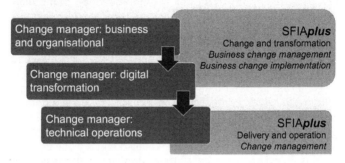

When is a role not a role?

It is worth mentioning here that change manager is being described as a role, not a job title. However, that does not mean that the role cannot exist as a job! It is easier to refer to it as a role for flexibility, so that it can be applied as a concept and fit according to size and scale of need. Some large organisations might have one or more change managers exclusively dedicated to change management; others might combine it with one or more other roles. Indeed, many small businesses may have an IT manager who is responsible for everything IT related, including technical change management.

The main message is that the functions of a change manager are important and should be assigned to someone, however large or small the operation.

SO, WHO IS THIS BOOK FOR?

The purpose of this book then, is to examine closely the role of the IT-specific change manager (henceforth referred to as change manager). It aims to clarify the role within the wider remit of organisational change and digital transformation, and demonstrate its existence at different levels of maturity, providing guidance on the establishment and continual improvement of the role.

It is suitable for a wide readership, including:

- current change managers looking for ways to benchmark their role and make improvements;

- aspiring change managers looking for insight into the role;

- change analysts considering their next move, or exploring the wider context of their role;

- business and digital transformation change managers looking for some demystification of the technical black box of operations;

- IT service managers looking for insight and ways in which to support all aspects of change for positive outcomes;

- IT service management students – or those learning about wider digital topics – to supplement studies, to gain some insight into the real world of the change manager and to help inform career direction decision-making;

- anyone considering a professional qualification in change management; for example, the BCS Specialist Certificate in Change Management.[2] Although this book is not a set text, it provides some context for the tasks at hand and may help to provide vicarious experience to support early practice;

---

2 https://certifications.bcs.org/category/15480

- anyone involved in the change life cycle, who is expected to work with a change manager and engage with the change management process. This includes members of the IT department, technical and management staff across all areas, from project management to service desk management, and business representatives of not just change but also business as usual.

GOOD PRACTICE AND PROFESSIONALISM

Best practice or good practice?

Somewhere during my career, 'best practice' gave way in popularity to 'good practice'. If we must distinguish between the two, 'good practice' suggests that there is always room for improvement whereas 'best practice' implies that a pinnacle of perfection has been reached.

'Best practice' also suggests that there are other practices that are inferior. Generically that may be the case, if you just made something up without standing on the shoulders of giants. On the other hand, if there is more than one accepted framework, best practice suggests favouritism.

The more you think about it, the more of a minefield it becomes and time is better spent putting it into practice than splitting hairs about its name. What you call it is a technicality; it is what you do that matters. Good practice is good enough.

> **Professionalism**
>
> Profession: a paid occupation, especially one involving training and a formal qualification.
>
> Professionalism: the competence or skill expected of a professional.
>
> (*Concise Oxford English Dictionary*)[3]

Best, or good, practice and professionalism are now well established in change management.

Process frameworks such as ITIL® and COBIT® are mature and the international standard for IT service management ISO 20000 was first published in 2005. The SFIA was launched in 2000 and has been updated regularly since, and BCS has adapted this as a career development tool for members in the form of SFIA**plus**, which is updated regularly with input from its membership to ensure that grass roots experience is always reflected.

Professional qualifications in IT change management are well established and run by a number of training providers, and mainstream formal education is beginning to recognise the importance of good practice IT service management as a foundation in IT-related roles. This can be seen in graduate and post-graduate modules at Higher Education level, and an increasing focus in apprenticeships and the forthcoming T Levels in UK Further Education (2020 onwards).[4]

BCS is a professional membership body, promoting formal change management training and qualifications, as well as opportunities to attend conferences, seminars and other continuing professional development (CPD) events.

---

3 *Concise Oxford English Dictionary* (2002). Oxford: Oxford University Press, p. 1141.

4 See www.gov.uk/government/news/new-t-levels-mark-a-revolution-in-technical-education

Special interest groups exist to share and build on good practice across the wide range of IT-related disciplines (in this case currently pitched at Business Change),[5] but if one doesn't exist for technical change management that is merely an opportunity for someone to take the lead!

This guide is intended to complement the wide range of information already available in technical IT (and general) change management, not repeat it. Where appropriate, reference is made for further reading in context; standards and frameworks are elaborated upon in a dedicated chapter, but not reinvented, and all are consolidated into a separate list at the end of this guide for easy reference. The book provides a starting point from which to enter the world of the change manager, with signposts to the good work that has already been done. Importantly, it is written from the human perspective, focusing on what it takes to make change management work and what it means to be a change manager. It is written for people about what they do, not what the process does.

WHY THIS BOOK WAS WRITTEN

As alluded to earlier, IT change management is often an afterthought, a case of closing the gate after the horse has bolted and seen as a necessary evil at worst, a process to be followed at best. Plenty has been written about process. But what about the people? Process doesn't happen by itself, and the change manager is more than just a job description.

This guide has been written to shine a light on the role of the change manager, in the illumination sense, to demystify what a change manager does, and, in the spotlight sense, to exemplify an often unsung champion of continuity and enabler of (rather than obstacle to) change.

The evolution of technical change in IT, and the difficulties associated with intervening in oncoming traffic, might make

---

5   See www.bcs.org/category/12139

change management seem like a poisoned chalice, but with its aim of balancing risks and maintaining progress it is more akin to a holy grail. By improving transparency and sharing real experiences, hints and tips in a variety of contexts, I hope this guide will help existing change managers, and analysts, to succeed in their remit and champion their cause.

For those considering a career in the field, I hope this guide will encourage you into what can be a rewarding position on the cusp between IT and business, and a career choice that can lead to a variety of opportunities in either.

THE STRUCTURE OF THIS BOOK

Going forwards then, this guide will explore the role of the change manager in the following way.

To set the scene, **Chapter 1** is an overview of the field: change management, and its position in the wider context of service management.

Chapter 2 covers a definition of the change manager role, including its purpose and objectives, knowledge, skills and behaviours, responsibilities, and close day-to-day interactions/interfaces with other roles and functions. This is consolidated with a pen portrait of the characteristics of a typical change manager.

Chapter 3 describes what a change manager does and **Chapter 4** describes how they do it. This is backed up in **Chapter 5** with descriptions of tools available to help fulfil the role, including the high-end, dedicated applications, but also pragmatic, make-do-and-mend ways to get started and prove the concept, or just get by at low cost.

Standards and frameworks are mentioned throughout where they might be relevant or helpful in context, but **Chapter 6** consolidates them to present the bigger picture and provide a one-stop-shop reference chapter.

Chapter 7 then places the change manager in the wider context of interfaces and dependencies across an organisation, which will expose some ideas, in **Chapter 8**, on where the role might lead you (or indeed, where transfer in from elsewhere might be the case).

Finally, case studies in **Chapter 9** explore the different levels of maturity of the role, from the ideal, well established, through the getting there, to the starting out, to show that the change manager is not necessarily born fully formed but can be a work in progress for the role-holder, as is the change management process for the organisation they belong to.

And on that note, I hope that anyone in, or going to, a change manager role will embrace it for the flux that it is at its heart, and as a journey rather than a destination. In the words of Heraclitus (*c.* 535—475 BCE), 'you can never step into the same river twice'.[6] Or, the only thing that is constant is change.

KEY POINTS

- This book is mainly about the change manager responsible for technical changes to IT infrastructure and services.

- Technical change management is designed to preserve the integrity of IT services and its principles are important in any organisation, large or small.

- This book aims to provide a way in to the role of change manager, referring to other related works as appropriate.

---

6   See www.britannica.com/biography/Heraclitus

1 OVERVIEW OF THE FIELD

This chapter sets the scene for technical change management by first introducing the wider discipline of IT service management, within which technical change management sits, and then going on to define change management itself and describe the purpose, benefits and some of the perceived problems and difficulties associated with the process.

INTRODUCTION TO IT SERVICE MANAGEMENT

IT service management, in the context of this book, refers to a comprehensive framework of good practice processes that work together to support the delivery of IT services. Proactive processes conspire to design and implement robust systems that resist failure, while reactive processes provide a safety net for when failure is unavoidable. Together they maintain the integrity of IT so that end-users can rely on its availability when they need it.

IT service management is a mature concept that has evolved over several decades and has drawn ideas and improvements from many private- and public-sector organisations. Its success has evolved into generic service management, with concepts adopted beyond IT services. The IT Infrastructure Library, or ITIL®, is a well-known IT service management framework, which, at the time of writing this guide, has begun its transformation into Version 4 (Foundation level manual and certification launched in February 2019 and more to follow.

For up-to-date information about ITIL®, see the Axelos website dedicated pages).[1]

IT + service + management

Instead of restating that which is better expressed elsewhere, I offer my own perspective on an industry that was born in my lifetime but whose absence might now be unthinkable.

In the late 1980s, IT was just IT. Most of its output came from a central function; few people had PCs, and personal devices were only beginning to emerge (the brick phone). The concept of IT as a service for others to operate came later. For me, the shift came with the advent of email and the impact it had on the communication possibilities of the international company I worked for at the time. It significantly reduced the need for travel and making calls at unsociable hours, and users embraced it for its function rather than its novelty.

Uptake was quick and IT service provision rapidly became a full-time job. This happened so fast that we didn't think about managing it at that stage. It was enough to keep up with demand as new technologies were adopted that transformed ways of working, and it was as much as we could manage just throwing down track ahead of the train. The first time the email system properly broke was the first time we stopped to look behind us, at which point the train ran us down.

Only at this point did we realise we must manage the service, not just provide the equipment, and as I progressed to new roles the world of ITIL® opened before

---

1   www.axelos.com/best-practice-solutions/itil

my eyes. This marked a turning point, when I stopped looking at IT from the bottom up and started looking at it from the top down. As a junior IT support manager in the foothills of IT service management, having a frame of reference gave me an invaluable perspective on the bigger picture and my relative position (and what was missing). I should point out that, to me then, IT service management meant ITIL®, and it still does. I should also point out that other frameworks are available, and the generic term IT Service Management (ITSM) reflects that.

IT service management is about the management of IT services; there are as many ways to do that as there are practitioners. ITSM refers to the body of knowledge that suggests how best to go about it, based on the accumulated experience of many practitioners over many years. At one end of the scale, it is just guidance; it is not compulsory; you don't have to do it all, or any of it, if it doesn't fit your needs and you can take your pick of what does. At the other end of the scale, it has been formalised into an international standard – ISO/IEC 20000 – in which compliance is implicit.

Whatever the requirement, as with many 'rules' it pays to understand them before you break them, in the interests of efficiency and not reinventing the wheel. To do anything other than stand on the shoulders of giants in the fast-paced world of technology is surely wilful neglect.

For a more comprehensive view of IT service management, its history, its aims and its processes, there are many frameworks to consider. These are introduced in more detail in **Chapter 6**, with pointers for further reading.

INTRODUCTION TO CHANGE MANAGEMENT

Change management is one of many IT service management processes. In ITIL®, it belongs to the Service Transition phase of the life cycle, but it is relevant from beginning to end. This section goes into more detail about change management and its pros and cons in IT governance.

What is change management?

ITIL® definition

'The process responsible for controlling the lifecycle of all changes, enabling beneficial changes to be made with minimum disruption to IT services.'[2]

In practice, change management means establishing a way for all technical changes to be identified centrally, at the initiation stage, before any work is done, and channelled consistently through transparent planning, testing, implementation and review.

At a high level it might look something like Figure 1.1.

The throughput of change will vary according to local needs and methods. For example, major software projects might deliver one big change in accordance with traditional waterfall development practice, or lots of small ones in line with an Agile approach; maintenance changes might align with supplier or manufacturer cycles or be bundled to fit a more tolerable schedule in the organisation. Fixes might be packaged and scheduled or depend on an alternative emergency process, but a strong ability to implement short-term workarounds might help to avoid that.

---

2 https://www.axelos.com/glossaries-of-terms

Figure 1.1 High level steps in a change management process

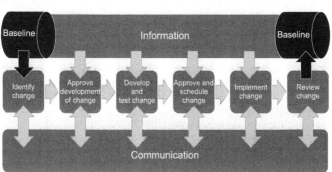

Why is it necessary?

Here are some good reasons for having a change management process:

- Central control of change provides an overview of needs, plans and costs so that they can be approved, prioritised and managed efficiently.
- Rigorous planning, testing and review help to ensure successful implementation.
- Sharing plans across IT and the business means that everyone knows **what** is happening **when** and can plan their own activity accordingly.
- Outputs from change management are inputs to other processes, which are more effective as a result.

In the smallest organisation with just one person making technical changes, there is still some value in outlining a definitive change management process. It saves time planning by providing a standard checklist starting place for each change; it ensures that nothing is accidentally missed that could potentially result in a problem during or after a change and it provides a baseline from which to improve, through review and revision of the process and its success in delivering change that works. Making mistakes is forgivable; making the same mistakes repeatedly is not.

In an organisation with more than one person making changes it becomes even more important, as a change management process will provide a consistent way of working for everyone to follow. It ensures that everything being done is out in the open so that all stakeholders can identify the impact of others' work on their own, it highlights potential conflicts and thus helps everyone to plan effectively.

In an organisation that is adopting other IT service management processes, change management is an important source of information without which the value of other processes can be curtailed. For example, incident and problem management make use of information about changes in their diagnosis; configuration management records are updated as a result of completed changes; and so on.

Furthermore, the processes embedded in ITSM generally, and ITIL® specifically, are the result of decades of practice, review and revision, sourced from practitioners across a wide spectrum of industry and services. They have evolved as technology and our dependency on it have developed. Change management is one of those processes and it is therefore safe to assume that it plays an important role in the delivery and management of IT services, or it wouldn't be included.

OK, it is necessary, but what are the benefits?

When we stop to think about it, the need for change management is obvious. It is about planning and executing technical change in such a way as to pre-empt any undesirable knock-on effects – things not working as they should after change has been applied, consequences not fully understood, preparation for all eventualities not made, delays restoring service after the fact. Whether from ignorance or blind optimism, the risks of proceeding without change management are too great.

The undesirable effects of change can derail business as usual. Those trying to get on with business can't and those trying to get on with something else get drawn back into problem solving and fire-fighting the fallout. Obviously, this is not good for business and the bottom line is that it costs money. Most of all, it is avoidable; that's why change management exists. To opt out of it knowing this is a risky strategy.

Benefits of change management include:

- reduces the risk of service downtime;
- reduces the need for business users to report service failures or experience interruption to their work;
- supports training and mobility across projects through use of consistent methods;
- pools expertise and sharing of knowledge through peer review;
- exposes information about change plans and schedules that can help to identify the cause of faults;
- provides updates to technical configuration records when changes take place to maintain a usable source of information for planning future changes;
- demonstrates a professional approach that inspires the confidence of end-users (without whom IT wouldn't be needed) and shows respect for their position;
- provides a well-oiled cog in the organisational machine – continual rehearsal ensures that IT is ready to support wider transformation and change projects.

Change management helps the business directly, in prevention and risk terms. But it also helps IT service management to manage other aspects of its work.

Sounds great, so what's the catch with change management?

The problem with change management is that it is often seen as interfering with the process of change itself. Change management takes time and forethought, things that can appear to be diametrically opposed to 'just getting on with it'. But it is time that might be spent anyway, if things go wrong; time that is already out of control in a fire-fighting situation when the loss-clock is ticking.

Time spent in consistent and quantifiable preparation is more manageable than time spent on unforeseen and therefore unquantifiable activity to restore the status quo. It is also time that the business-end of the organisation is largely protected from. But it can be perceived as a vicious circle. When technical staff are busy fire-fighting and responding to demand, change management is a frustration that will slow progress up front, and this sometimes presents a conflict of interests for people who are being pulled in two directions: to do it now or to do it well.

Change management slows down progress up front because it requires cooperation. It stands to reason that one person being their own master is quicker and therefore more desirable than following a process, which curtails spontaneity and brings you face to face with departmental silos; autonomy is removed, and it may feel as though technical ability is being questioned. A good process crosses departmental boundaries, but such openness can sometimes be at odds with local culture and politics. It is important, at the same time as demanding consistency, to respect differences and recognise the need for flexibility when it is required.

Implementing change management

Implementing change management means disrupting the ways in which individuals already work. Understandably, they may be happy with their methods and not disposed to changing them. Individuals make work happen, and individuals are, well, individual! It is a problem that is not unique to change management, but a problem to be resolved, nevertheless. Crucially, it is not enough to circulate some instructions and expect change management to happen. The gap between the desired ideal and messy reality must be closed, and it is in this respect that a good change manager is invaluable.

The difficulties alluded to are not insurmountable, but they do mean that change management can exist at different levels of maturity. The prevailing culture will determine the level of resistance and it can be a struggle in choppy waters where doing it properly is directly at odds with the need for immediate action in an already imperfect situation. There may be wider process issues, perceived lack of need versus cost issues, skills and knowledge to develop in all participants, perhaps management commitment to influence. This all takes time, so implementation might feel like a drawn-out process at best, and one that is making no progress at worst. But no one said that doing something worthwhile is necessarily easy, and overcoming difficulties only improves the satisfaction of success!

More about making it work later.

KEY POINTS

- The benefits of technical change management are established – dismiss them at your peril.
- Implementing change management can be difficult because it usually means getting people to change how they work.
- Change management is never dull!

2 THE CHANGE MANAGER ROLE

This chapter explores the role of the change manager, why it exists, what is involved and where it fits into the greater scheme of IT and organisational change.

WHICH CAME FIRST, THE CHANGE OR THE CHANGE MANAGER?

Change tends to just happen. If you are very forward thinking when planning your very first IT installation (and lucky enough to be there), you might consider the likelihood of future change and create the role of change manager from the beginning. In reality, this is unlikely to have happened, not least because it costs money to create a role in anticipation of a future need and the practical truth is that there are usually enough things to do with resources today without spending them on tomorrow.

Quite often things just evolve. Infrastructures grow, software updates come out, upgrades become necessary, technology advances in ways not previously considered and, before you know it, change is happening and is its own master. This might carry on for a while with no consequences, but sooner or later something will clash with something else or something will fail, and overnight (or over the weekend) technical change can become a bad thing for managers and users, who, understandably, want to know what went wrong, why and, inevitably, whose fault it is.

It may be at this stage that the idea of 'change management' is first introduced. For this reason, change management is usually playing catch-up with change that is already off and running, which also means that the role of the change manager must be applied after change has established its own way(s) of working – ways, plural, when there can be as many variations as there are people involved in unmanaged change.

The first change to arrive always has the easiest time. If you are lucky enough to be starting at the dawn of the first change, then you have an opportunity to call the shots before a multitude of other ways of working emerge and attempt to co-exist. If you are working in an organisation that has mature processes, tools and culture in respect of change management, more than likely some pain has been gone through already. If you are, like many of us, trying to put a stick in the spokes of a turning wheel without crashing anything, then I hope you will forgive yourself for feeling disheartened from time to time and take heart from a pragmatic approach to change management and a practical guide to making it work. Change management is inherently difficult to implement because necessity often precedes forethought, but the good news is that the more established it becomes as a concept, the more normalised the behaviours associated with it become; there are ways of smoothing the impact of enforced change to process, as we shall see.

Given the different possibilities, then, it is reasonable to expect the change manager role to exist at different levels of maturity according to the prevailing culture. So, as well as considering the fully functioning ideal change manager, this BCS guide also aims to reflect the different stages of a developing change management function – as a way of helping change managers to locate themselves and their contexts in terms of the target, but also as a way of demonstrating that any change management is better than no change management at all, and continual improvement is more realistic than instant perfection.

Getting people to change the way they like to do things individually in order to cooperate in a common process is rarely instant and changing the status quo will not happen overnight. But it is not necessary to impose a rigid and prescriptive change management process as a one-size-fits-no one solution, when continual improvement offers a more inclusive approach that respects others' ideas, preferences and knowledge. Buy-in comes with collaboration, and taking the slow road often gets

11

you there quicker. One step at a time, with everyone on board, is more reliable than lip-service to a notional process that people try to bypass, and risks are more manageable with full control.

Continual improvement

Continual improvement refers to the cycle of activity whereby the effect of doing something is monitored to identify changes that can be made to get a better result next time. It is a dynamic approach to implementation that allows perfection to be a target to aspire to, rather than an unachievable starting place. It is dynamic and responsive, rather than rigid and presumptuous.

It is often referred to as the Deming Cycle: Plan, Do, Study, Act[1] (also known as Plan, Do, Check, Act) and is a generic process with wide application.

Continual vs continuous

These two words are often used interchangeably. The *Oxford English Dictionary*[2] says:

Continual: constantly or frequently occurring.

Continuous: without interruption.

Which one is correct is no doubt an area of debate, according to intended meaning, context and preference. I prefer 'continual' for the activities carried out by humans to improve how a process works, because they are periodic and humans are known to sleep at times. Automated monitoring and adjustment of a computerised process, for example, might be 'continuous'.

---

1   See https://deming.org/explore/p-d-s-a

2   *Concise Oxford English Dictionary* (2002). Oxford: Oxford University Press. p. 308.

PURPOSE OF THE CHANGE MANAGER ROLE

The change manager role exists to own and manage the change management process.

From a strategic perspective, this might mean defining and implementing the process and tools; once that has been done, it means running it day to day. This could include managing change analysts if it is a large operation; configuring and administering tools; advising participants on process requirements, both generally and in the context of specific changes; coordinating communications; approving changes; producing schedules; arranging and chairing meetings; updating records; producing reports; and generally having a finger in every pie from which technical change is forthcoming. How much or how little this amounts to will depend on the size of the organisation and the throughput of change.

The change management process exists to provide checks and balances so that changes carried out are done so with minimal risk. Part of that is to enable rigorous planning and testing by defining the process through which all changes must go. The change manager is responsible for ensuring the quality of those inputs and thus fulfils a quality assurance role. In addition, the change manager takes an overview of all change. An individual or project manager will focus on their own changes, without necessarily being aware of the bigger change picture. The change manager is positioned as a filter through which all plans go, to be synthesised into a master plan that can be assessed for overall risk and shared so that everyone knows what is happening and when. The change manager role is the focal point and gatekeeper for technical change.

It is important to recognise that the change management process cannot run itself. It might be tempting to install a change management software solution and have someone configure it, with the idea that everyone does their own thing according to some rules. But without an owner the process will break down. Even if the system is used religiously by change-makers who maintain their own records and have their colleagues peer review them, intervention is still required to coordinate the inputs and outputs of the process, and facilitate the communication and decision-making that must take place between stakeholders across IT and the business. There will be clashing priorities and emergency changes. There will be changes that are controversial and changes that need to be made in a less than ideal world. And the essence of the process is decision-making based on risk, which someone must do or facilitate – depending on how big the risk is! The change manager will have a remit within which they are authorised to act autonomously on the available information; beyond that, they must know where the buck stops and seek appropriate intervention.

The change manager role is pivotal. The change manager is the glue that keeps the change management process together and the oil that keeps it moving. It might be full-time, it might be part-time, it might involve some extra duties someone didn't bargain for, it might even be called something else, but if a change management process is necessary, a change manager is necessary too.

Role vs job title

It is worth stating, again, that change manager is described in this guide as a role, but it can also be a job title. If there is sufficient churn to justify a full-time change manager, then it is unlikely to be a controversial decision to have a job called 'change manager', but those with a smaller need must not be deterred from applying the concept in a part-time context. The role, in this sense, can be attributed to someone's job, alongside other duties. But it is important to recognise what is involved so that it can be given appropriate resources (and recognition) to ensure that it is fulfilled adequately. Consideration should also be given to conflicts of interest, as perceptions of partiality can have a negative effect.

RESPONSIBILITIES, KNOWLEDGE, SKILLS AND BEHAVIOURS

This section draws on the levels of responsibility in the change management process identified in SFIA, and the knowledge, skills and behaviours applied in SFIA*plus*. The aim is to add value by extrapolating what this means for the change manager role.

Responsibilities

As the change management process owner, the change manager is responsible for everything relating to the successful operation of the process.

At the very least, this will include managing, maintaining and continually improving the change management process, and making sure that everyone required to participate is competent in the workings of the process and its supporting tools. It might also mean implementing a change management process, if one does not exist.

On a day-to-day basis, the change manager is responsible for enabling technical change in a way that does not unduly disrupt the working of the organisation or put it at risk, either directly, as a result of a failed change, or indirectly, as a result of external factors such as breached security. 'Enabling' is a key word here; blocking changes should not be necessary, since the process should ensure that required changes are approved for development before work starts.

However, given that the intervention of a process might be regarded as getting in the way of change, the change manager is already challenged to avoid the perception of blocking. They are responsible, therefore, for running a fit-for-purpose, but lean and dynamic, operation that is unhindered by bureaucracy and is flexible when it needs to be. They are also responsible for publicising the fact if they want to make the most of it.

SFIA and SFIA*plus*

The detailed responsibilities of a role determine the specific knowledge, skills and behaviours required and these are defined for change management in SFIA and SFIA***plus***, and are updated regularly to stay in line with industry practice.

SFIA describes seven levels of responsibility that apply generically to all disciplines. Each level is described in terms of autonomy, influence, complexity, knowledge and business skills involved. The tasks performed in each discipline are described specifically at the levels that apply in each case (not all levels apply to all disciplines), beneath an overall definition of the discipline. Table 2.1 shows how SFIA aligns the discipline of change management with these levels.

Table 2.1 SFIA levels of responsibility for change management[3]

Change Management (CHMG)

The management of change to the service infrastructure including service assets, configuration items and associated documentation. Change management uses requests for change (RFC) for standard or emergency changes and changes due to incidents or problems to provide effective control and reduction of risk to the availability, performance, security and compliance of the business services impacted by the change.

SFIA responsibility level	Application
1. Follow	Not applicable
2. Assist	Documents changes based on requests for change. Applies change control procedures.

(Continued)

---

[3] www.sfia-online.org/en/framework/sfia-7/skills/service-management/service-transition/change-management

Table 2.1 (Continued)

SFIA responsibility level	Application
3. Apply	Develops, documents and implements changes based on requests for change. Applies change control procedures.
4. Enable	Assesses, analyses, develops, documents and implements changes based on requests for change.
5. Ensure, advise	Develops implementation plans for complex requests for change. Evaluates risks to the integrity of service environment inherent in proposed implementations (including availability, performance, security and compliance of the business services impacted). Seeks authority for those activities, reviews the effectiveness of change implementation, suggests improvement to organisational procedures governing change management. Leads the assessment, analysis, development, documentation and implementation of changes based on requests for change.
6. Initiate, influence	Sets the organisation's policy for the management of change in live services and test environments. Ensures effective control and treatment of risk to the availability, performance, security and compliance of the business services impacted.
7. Set strategy, inspire, mobilise	Not applicable

BCS has developed SFIA into SFIA*plus*, adding information about typical work activities, detailed knowledge, skills and behaviours, appropriate training, personal development activities and qualifications to each level defined in SFIA, to provide a comprehensive career planning tool for BCS members.

It is important to note that SFIA and SFIA*plus* are both organised by discipline (change management), not role (change manager); junior and senior roles can be inferred from the levels, but there is not necessarily a strict ratio of one role to one level because the levels relate to discrete activities. If we say that all levels need to be fulfilled to complete the change management discipline, this might be achieved through one or more roles, overseen by a change manager, depending on the organisation.

Table 2.2 summarises the SFIA*plus* change management activities into one table, consolidated to remove overlap and group similar types of activity together. They are shown in alphabetical order for ease of reference; no weighting of priority or importance is implied. This view may be helpful in planning any delegation of tasks.

Table 2.2 Consolidated view of SFIA*plus* change management activities at levels 2, 3, 4, 5 and 6

Activity	Details	Level
Awareness	Assists with the provision of awareness material to clients/users to explain the importance of a structured change management process.	3, 4
	Promotes awareness of the importance of a structured change management process, working with other service management functions to ensure effective operation of the change management function and the consistency of procedures.	5, 6

(Continued)

Table 2.2 (Continued)

Activity	Details	Level
Database	Transcribes data onto the change management database, ensuring accuracy and consistency of data.	2, 3
	Carries out simple enquiries on the status of changes, using the change database where appropriate.	3
	Logs requests for change (RFCs) on the change management database, ensuring accuracy and consistency of data.	4
	Maintains the client/user database.	4
	Administers the change management database, ensuring accuracy and consistency of data.	5
Documentation	Assists with the documentation of approved changes in accordance with RFC and approval documentation.	2
	Circulates change documentation to a defined distribution of clients/users.	2, 3, 4
Information	Responds to queries from clients/users and contacts clients/users (for whom a change management service is provided) to raise queries and provide information, entering details on to the client/user database where appropriate.	3, 4

(Continued)

Table 2.2 (Continued)

Activity	Details	Level
	Progresses status of changes with service departments to ensure that data is current.	4
	Provides advice to clients/users on the impact of requests for change and ensures that the appropriate impact analyses are carried out before changes are authorised.	5, 6
	Provides management information and statistics on the progress of changes to senior management and clients/users, including performance against service level agreements.	5
Management	Tracks, and may assist with the implementation of, approved changes in accordance with RFC and approval documentation.	3
	Manages changes to the live service environment, taking account of priorities and other changes that may impact on service availability, security and safety. Provides advice to users on the system of prioritisation and the likely timescales for implementation.	5

(Continued)

Table 2.2 (Continued)

Activity	Details	Level
Meetings	Acts as secretary to meetings that review changes, such as change advisory boards (CABs).	4
	Chairs meetings that review changes, such as CABs, ensuring that changes are expedited to maintain the required infrastructure.	5, 6
Reporting	Interrogates the client/user database to produce reports for bodies that review changes, such as change advisory boards CABs, and for clients and management.	4, 5
Review	Facilitates regular assessments, reviews and audits of the change management process, taking ownership of the findings and expediting action to close gaps.	5, 6
Schedules	Assists with the production of schedules of RFCs for managing changes to the live environment.	3, 4
System	Contributes to the evaluation or establishment of the change management system, ensuring conformance to documentation standards. Maintains the change management system in accordance with agreed procedures.	5

SFIA***plus*** provides the full specifications for each level of the change management discipline, including the generic attributes, work activities, knowledge, skills and behaviours, training, personal development activities and qualifications – details are on the BCS website.[4]

It should also be noted that some of the activities, mostly at the lower levels, are likely to be carried out by participants in the change management process, not the change manager (or their staff). For example, logging requests for change should normally be done by those planning and implementing change. The change manager may support this, but they are ultimately only responsible for it being done.

Knowledge, skills and behaviours

If the change manager is responsible for every level of change management activity, it might follow that the knowledge, skills and behaviours expected of a change manager should be an accumulation of the knowledge, skills and behaviours from all levels. In this case, a change manager at level 6 should inherit the knowledge, skills and behaviours of a change manager at level 5 and so on.

Knowledge and skills

SFIA***plus*** conflates 'knowledge' and 'skills' in an overall description of each requirement and, like 'continual' and 'continuous', the two words are often used interchangeably.

I briefly lifted the lid on the can of worms that is a definition of these terms and concluded that knowledge may or may not include skills. In the practical work context, very generally, I think of 'knowledge' as knowing how to do something and 'skill' as being able to do it,

---

4   https://rolemodel.bcs.org/BrowseSFIAPlus

in which case a belt and braces approach to holding up these particular trousers is appropriate.

It is reasonable to expect that, between them, all those involved in delivering change management have the appropriate knowledge and skills for their level, so conflating the terms in the SFIA*plus* skills framework avoids any doubt that both are required and ensures that everyone interprets the requirement fully. Indeed, the difference between a failed and a successful process may lie in the gap between knowing how it works and being able to work it.

Tables 2.3, 2.4 and 2.5 show the combined and summarised knowledge, skills and behaviours for change management levels 2–6 as described in SFIA*plus*. Together, they should represent the core attributes that a senior change manager has accumulated in their rise to the top of the field.

Technical knowledge and skills

Table 2.3 Change manager technical knowledge and skills derived from SFIA*plus* change management

---

Knowledge and skills – technical

Change management	The management of change to the service infrastructure including service assets, configuration items and associated documentation. Change management uses RFCs for standard or emergency changes to provide effective control and reduction of risk to the availability, performance, security and compliance of the business services subject to change.

(Continued)

Table 2.3 (Continued)

Knowledge and skills – technical

Configuration management	The control of IT assets (configuration items), including hardware, software, licences, documentation and any other component required to deliver an IT service.
Release management	The management of the processes, systems and functions to package, build, test and deploy application changes and updates.
Metrics	The collection, analysis and application of historical and synthetic measurements in the estimation of IT activities.
Structured reviews	Methods and techniques for structured reviews, including reviews of technical work products, test plans, business cases, architectures and any other key deliverables.
Database software	Software that enables the user to create, populate and manipulate data structures.
Operational/service architecture	Knowledge of the IT infrastructure and the IT applications and service processes used.
IT environment	The IT environment relating to own sphere of work including own organisation customers, suppliers and partners.

(Continued)

Table 2.3 (Continued)

Knowledge and skills – technical

Business environment	The business environment relating to own sphere of work including own organisation customers, suppliers and partners.
Own organisation's products and services	The products and/or services supplied to customers by own organisation.
Collaborative software systems	The use of social networking technology to improve collaboration and community communication within organisations.

The technical knowledge and skills shown in Table 2.3 relate to the core topics of IT change management, in the sense of technology itself that is subject to change, and in the technicalities of the process of change management.

There will probably be a change management software tool that underpins the process, for creating requests for change at least, and this might be part of an integrated IT service management tool leveraging other processes.

The change management process commonly overlaps with configuration and release management and a working knowledge of these additional ITSM processes is useful. Configuration records (should) underpin the specification of changes so that planning and risk management are carried out against validated information. Release management relates to the building and testing of software and hardware that might be done cyclically and is a cog within the change management machine. Both processes are described fully in ITIL® Service Transition.[5]

---

5 www.tsoshop.co.uk/AXELOS-Global-Best-Practice/ITIL/#Service-Transition

Understanding how the IT and business environments are supported by technology is important for the change manager who will be managing changes against it; and knowing how this relates to the organisation's services and products is an essential part of that awareness. The change manager must make an independent judgement on the impact and risks involved in change and being able to systematically review requests for change will be part of the change manager's approach to quality assurance that is carried out with others participating throughout the process.

Techniques and tools for monitoring, measuring and reporting the change management process will be required to demonstrate its status and continual improvement, and the ability to make effective use of communication tools will be invaluable in maintaining the profile of the process and managing the day-to-day activities and workflow.

General knowledge and skills

Table 2.4 Change manager general knowledge and skills derived from SFIA*plus* change management

Knowledge and skills – general

Legislation	Relevant national and international legislation.
Operations management	Methods, techniques and tools for planning, organising, resourcing, directing, coordinating and monitoring ongoing (non-project) activities.
Techniques for effective meetings	Methods and techniques for running effective meetings and for understanding and influencing the roles played by participants.
Risk management	Methods and techniques for the assessment and management of business risk, including safety-related risk.

(Continued)

Table 2.4 (Continued)

Knowledge and skills – general

Customer service techniques	Techniques for identifying, gathering and validating customer needs in the delivery of IT services.
Quality management	The system or method for the management of quality within the employing organisation's (general or IT) practices.
Document management techniques	Methods and techniques for the organisation, storage and version control of information.

Table 2.4 describes the more generalised knowledge and skills pertaining to the change manager role. These transfer to and from other disciplines but nevertheless are required by the rounded change manager.

Managing the workload, the process and the people, across teams, departments and business areas, will require strong operational management, document management and meeting management skills. Since changes are ultimately for end-users or customers, customer service, too, plays an important role. If any IT people lack in this area the change manager must make up for the deficit, as their role is largely to negate any undesirable impact on customers and the services they need for their business.

Knowledge of legislation will be both generic and specific. Any change manager should be familiar with legislation protecting health and safety, since the priority and planning of changes must give this the highest importance. Changes facilitating accessibility should also be treated with respect and, conversely, changes that undermine accessibility, for all or for one, should be identified and revised accordingly. Equal rights legislation is therefore fundamental to maintaining a fair and legal workplace and technical change represents a risk in this respect.

Additionally, there may be industry-specific legislation that must be taken into account for change management; for example, in financial services and pharmaceuticals industries. Standards such as ISO 9001 for quality management might be used to manage compliance with legislation, amongst other things. If there is no organisational quality management process in which to embed change management, the change manager will need to consider their own methods to manage continual improvement. Relevant standards are considered more closely in **Chapter 6**.

Risk management is foundational to the change process and must factor in compliance with legislation alongside every other threat to services and organisational survival. Techniques can be drawn from quality management approaches and also project management.

Behaviours

Table 2.5 Change manager behaviours derived from SFIA*plus* change management

Behaviours

Conceptual thinking	Acquiring understanding of the underlying issues in complex problems or situations by correctly relating these to simpler or better understood concepts, models or previous experiences.
Strategic perspective	Keeping overall objectives and strategies in mind, and not being unduly preoccupied by matters of detail.
Organisational awareness	Understanding the hierarchy and culture of own, customer and supplier organisations and being able to identify the decision makers and influencers.

(Continued)

Table 2.5 (Continued)

Behaviours	
Influence, persuasion and personal impact	The ability to convey a level of confidence and professionalism, positively influencing and persuading others to take a specific course of action when there is no direct line of command or control.
Providing direction	Directing others to undertake specified tasks.
Follow-up and monitoring	Checking progress against targets, reporting and escalating exceptions/issues as necessary, and acting to resolve exceptions.
Planning and organisation	Determining a course of action by breaking it down into smaller steps and by planning and resourcing each of these, making allowance for potential problems.
Decision-making	Making decisions at the appropriate time, taking into account the needs of the situation, priorities, constraints, known risks, and availability of necessary information and resources.
Interacting with people	Establishing relationships and maintaining contacts with people from a variety of backgrounds and disciplines. Effective, approachable and sensitive communicator in different societies and cultures.
Leadership	Identifying goals and objectives, and motivating and leading others towards their achievement.
Delegation	Delegating tasks, responsibilities and authorities effectively.

(Continued)

Table 2.5 (Continued)

Behaviours	
Analytical thinking	Acquiring a proper understanding of a problem or situation by breaking it down systematically into its component parts and identifying the relationships between these parts; selecting the appropriate method/tool to resolve the problem; and reflecting critically on the result, so that what is learned is identified and assimilated.
Information acquisition	Identifying gaps in the available information required to understand a problem or situation and devising a means of resolving them.
Flexibility	Taking account of new information, changed circumstances or business requirements and modifying response to a problem or situation accordingly.
Cross-functional and inter-disciplinary awareness	Understanding the needs, objectives and constraints of those in other disciplines and functions.
Customer focus	Understanding the needs of the internal or external customer and regularly checking with the customer when taking actions or making decisions.
Initiative	Being proactive, anticipating opportunities for service improvement and taking appropriate action.
Attention to detail	Applying appropriate quality standards to all tasks undertaken and ensuring that nothing is overlooked.

(Continued)

Table 2.5 (Continued)

Behaviours

Teamwork	Working collaboratively (rather than competitively) with others to achieve a common goal.
Numeracy	Acquiring understanding of the metrics associated with a problem or situation, their significance and relationship, and being able to manipulate these as necessary to identify solutions.
Persistence	Meeting targets and fulfilling agreements even when adverse circumstances prevail.
Written expression	Communicating effectively in writing.

The behaviours listed in Table 2.5 represent the soft skills that the change manager will need; the ways of doing things; and the quality of the actions around performing the more clearly defined, measurable activities that demonstrate technical and general knowledge and skills.

It is probably no accident that this is the longest of the three lists and it is probably fair to say that they are the hardest won attributes. Many will be developed over the course of experience, with exposure to success and failures in equal measure to drill and practice. Rather than justify them in context, I invite you to reflect instead on what they say about the role and to make their continual refinement your aim, for they will stand you in good stead in any senior role.

Further reading

SFIA*plus* provides detailed descriptions of knowledge and skills across the five levels of responsibility for change management with the addition of required depth at four further levels:

- aware of;
- familiar with;
- proficient in;
- expert in.

CONTEXT OF THE ROLE

The change manager stands firmly in the IT department, but at the perimeter, facing out as well as in. They may be responsible for managing one or more change analysts directly but the work they are involved with is mostly owned by others.

Technical change is carried out by technical people. There might be a large number of technical people from different disciplines or, at the other extreme, just one person responsible for everything, depending on the size of the organisation and the nature of the change. They might be inside the same IT department as the change manager or belong to one or more external organisations delivering services or projects. A complete change may be made up of one or more individual changes that cross jurisdictions and may be coordinated as part of a project. Anyone in an IT department might be eligible to make changes, or they might be confined to a core team supporting live operations.

One way or another, technical change is carried out on behalf of the business. Some changes might be the result of internal IT department identification; for example, fixes, upgrades and maintenance changes. Others might have been initiated by specific business areas for new or improved services, or at the organisational top level as part of a bigger transformation, and everywhere in between.

The change manager owns the change management process, but generally none of the changes it manages. They monitor the efficiency and effectiveness of the process using data about the changes that go through it and their successes and failures. But other than that, effectively, the change manager interferes with everyone else's business. There is, of course, one exception, and that is where changes relate to the change management system, but this is hardly the bread and butter of the job. The system is there to manage the work of others in terms of risk to the status quo.

The change manager, therefore, works with a wide range of people in other roles both inside and outside the IT department and the organisation: IT technical and managerial staff, project managers, change and transformation leaders, departmental heads, business users, and third-party suppliers and service providers. It is a truly pivotal role and the interfaces and dependencies in relation to it are covered in detail in **Chapter 7**.

PORTRAIT OF A CHANGE MANAGER

Roles and responsibilities, knowledge, skills and behaviours are all necessary in defining the requirements of a change manager, but they present a somewhat fragmented picture. Who fulfills the role of a change manager? What are they like? Where did they come from? How do the knowledge, skills and behaviours translate into the characteristics of a change manager?

A change manager will need to have a good understanding of where change management sits in the overarching IT service management function so is likely to have some relevant training and direct experience at a managerial level. That might come from inside IT, or from working closely with IT service delivery from the business side, backed up with broad IT service management qualifications that expose the bigger picture and purpose. As a service management evangelist, a change manager will champion the need for control of the whole; they will be a team player, not a maverick.

They will also require an overview of the IT services estate and how it relates to the business, including operational peaks and troughs, and service priorities through the business life cycle in each department. Forensic detail is not necessary, but a mental image of what the organisation is trying to achieve, and when, will help to set the tone for good planning and management, and command the respect of business leaders. Although attention to detail is important at the change end of the job, the change manager will take a strategic view of the role of IT, not a partisan one. They will know and act for the business.

They will need to have a good process head, working with representatives from IT teams and business departments to get the right people involved at the right stages, and to configure and operate the process tools. They should know how any software tools they use work and should understand their features. It may not be necessary to roll up sleeves and configure them if one-off implementation is a specialised skill set hired in from a supplier, but ideally the change manager should be master of their own destiny. They should be able to administer their own system or have unfettered access to someone who can. However, carrying out the maintenance of the infrastructure that supports the system should be necessary only in a situation where the change manager role is combined with other technical responsibilities; for example, in a very small organisation. Either way, changes required must be subject to the change process just like anything else, and without any shortcuts or preferential treatment!

Impartiality should go without saying but sometimes it can be difficult to maintain appropriate checks and balances, so conflicts of interest should be avoided to prevent accidental breaches of process. This is especially true when the change manager role is assigned to someone in addition to their normal day job. Anyone whose job includes hands-on implementation or maintenance activities ideally should not be the change manager as well. They would, in effect, be marking their own homework. That might not be a huge problem, if outcomes suggest that the change management process is doing its job adequately, but in a situation where proof of compliance is needed it would be difficult to demonstrate this to an auditor, so conflict is best avoided. The configuration manager, too, should not be doubled up with the change manager role, because configuration management data can be used to identify change management breaches. Control of both roles risks manipulation. That is not to suggest that someone would want to do this but only that it can be difficult to prove that they haven't, which makes evidence for process compliance questionable and puts audits at risk.

Good communication skills are fundamental to the change manager role. They will need to discuss change at technical and non-technical levels. They should be as comfortable in the business arena as they are in the technical back-office; fluent in both languages and able to provide translation each way. As a one-person PR machine, they will need to be confident speaking to senior business representatives and senior IT colleagues. Not only will they need to justify their position articulately in writing and face to face, they will also need to make sure that everything going through the process is articulated clearly as well. Written records are the foundation upon which all changes are assessed. They must be clear and comprehensive, and understandable to everyone involved in decision-making, and the change manager is the gatekeeper of quality in this respect.

Along with good communication skills go confidence and the ability to lead, influence and persuade. When having to say no is sometimes necessary, it is vital to have the courage of conviction. The ability to analyse a situation and draw conclusions will provide the foundation for confidence and the conviction to argue a case when necessary. Subtler skills can also be useful to help the change manager gain the cooperation of those who not only have no line-management obligations to them, but also usually know more about the technical details of a change than the change manager. Even with a technical background, a change manager is unlikely to be an expert in everything and so needs to be able to demonstrate the value of breadth over depth in their reasoning. Experience of working in matrix-managed organisations, where individuals have multiple reporting lines, can provide helpful confidence in handling potentially conflicting demands.

Brokering the broad spectrum of IT also means brokering a broad range of opinions, priorities and stakes. The change manager will be a meeting manager to ensure that agreements are reached, and they will have a secretariat function to ensure that outcomes are recorded. A fundamental part of the change management process is the CAB, which is the coming together of stakeholder representatives. Stakeholders in change will vary with subject; stakeholders in business and IT operations will have permanent seats and perhaps variable attendance, provided each area is represented by someone empowered to participate fully. Meetings need to be scheduled, agendas prepared, outcomes noted and minutes organised for the record. The change manager must be someone with the gravitas to facilitate a decision as well as contribute to it, but also be comfortable with the 'paperwork' that is inevitable in the administrative side of the role. Technical and administrative work are not mutually exclusive, but that does not necessarily make them an agreeable combination, and it may be a rare breed that embraces both.

When described as pivotal, it is perhaps stating the obvious that a change manager must face outwards in many directions and be convincing in all of them – a jack of all trades but master of the process. On that basis, the change manager could come from anywhere if they have the aptitude and interest. Maturity, and the ability to get up to speed on business and infrastructure quickly, can outweigh any one specialism. Credibility is perhaps the most important quality, in equal measures of business acumen and technical understanding, to earn respect for their contribution from all sides.

How much technical knowledge does a change manager need?

If the details of changes are being provided by the people with the technical skills to design them, is it necessary for the change manager to have technical knowledge as well? There are pros and cons for being a 'non-technical' change manager.

Change requests must be understandable for everyone in the review and approval process, and this includes non-technical people. Having a non-technical change manager puts in place an automatic filter, to make sure that not too much technical jargon escapes to make them unintelligible outside IT. On the other hand, technical people often don't like to be questioned by people they perceive to know less than them about their subject, so being non-technical could be a barrier to cooperation.

This might lead the change manager to dismiss the detail on trust, but this undermines their assurance role and weakens the process. One way of dealing with this could be to pre-empt the sharp end of the process and ask to participate in planning meetings, in the interests of developing technical knowledge and demonstrating interest. Alternatively, they could ask specialists for recommended reading or do their own research and ask for verification. Importantly, all options show a willingness to learn and a level of humility that will feel less threatening to experts.

What this really means is that the change manager must have some degree of technical knowledge to be able to understand enough about the changes they are managing. The ability to gain credibility in this respect can make or break a change manager. Having a lack of technical knowledge shouldn't get in the way of the job, slow down the process or waste people's time. Although they are not expected to be master of everything, they will need to demonstrate sufficient knowledge in every area. A change manager can come from a non-technical discipline, but they will need to take the initiative in plugging their knowledge gaps.

KEY POINTS

- The change manager owns and manages the change management process, but they must also be able to manage the people involved, with or without direct authority.

- The change manager plays a pivotal role that touches all areas of IT and the business.

- By definition, change management is emblematic of flux and a change manager must be comfortable with their own continual evolution of knowledge.

3 CHANGE MANAGER ACTIVITIES

Chapter 2 described the SFIA*plus* activities performed in change management at five levels of seniority (SFIA level 2 to level 6). These represent activities that are carried out by all participants in the process, not just the change manager. Table 2.2 showed the merged levels as an overview of all activities, with duplication removed.

This chapter further consolidates the process, to distil an ordered view and separate the activities typically carried out by the change manager from those usually performed elsewhere. The aim is to clarify a typical change manager role, without losing sight of the whole, so that the role can be scaled according to local need and the line fall where necessary.

To demonstrate this, Table 3.1 shows the contents of Table 2.2 regrouped into subject areas to develop some structure. The shaded rows represent activities that process participants – other than the change manager – might also be expected to do. Typically, they would be IT technical staff and managers involved in preparing and implementing changes. Some activities may be wholly allocated to the change manager (or change analysts under their direction), such as circulating change documentation or managing queries. Others are more likely to remain the responsibility of those making the changes; for example, logging requests for change and implementing approved changes.

Checks and balances

If the change manager is in the position of defining and implementing changes, the process should allow for wide enough scrutiny and approval to ensure that the benefits of the process are fully realised. In other words: marking your own homework defeats the purpose of the process!

Table 3.1 An approximation of the activities of a change manager adapted from SFIA*plus* change management levels 2–6 with activities not exclusively performed by the change manager shaded grey

Activity	Details	Level
Change management process	Sets the change management policy. Evaluates or establishes the change management system, implementing improvements where necessary. Maintains the change management system in accordance with agreed procedures, ensuring conformance to documentation standards. This includes a process for emergency changes.	6
	Promotes awareness of the importance of a structured change management process, working with other service management functions to ensure effective operation of the change management function and the consistency of procedures.	5, 6

(Continued)

Table 3.1 (Continued)

Activity	Details	Level
Process operation	Maintains the client/user database.	4
	Administers the change management database, ensuring accuracy and consistency of data.	5
	Acts as secretary to meetings that review changes, such as CABs.	4
	Chairs meetings that review changes, such as CABs, ensuring that changes are expedited to maintain the required infrastructure.	5, 6
	Assists with the production of schedules of RFCs for managing changes to the live environment.	3, 4
	Transcribes data on to the change management database, ensuring accuracy and consistency of data.	2, 3
	Logs RFCs on the change management database, ensuring accuracy and consistency of data.	4
	Circulates change documentation to a defined distribution of clients/users.	2, 3, 4
	Assists with the documentation of approved changes in accordance with RFC and approval documentation.	2

(Continued)

Table 3.1 (Continued)

Activity	Details	Level
	Carries out simple enquiries on the status of changes, using the change database where appropriate.	3
	Analyses incidents and problems, and determines trends, initiating preventive action to minimise the likelihood of recurrence.	6
	Advises clients/users on the impact of RFCs and ensures that the appropriate impact analyses are carried out before changes are authorised.	6
Change implementation	Tracks and may assist with the implementation of approved changes in accordance with RFC and approval documentation.	3
	Manages (major) changes to the live service environment, taking account of priorities and other changes that may impact on service availability, security and safety. Provides advice to users on the system of prioritisation and the likely timescales for implementation.	5 (6)
	Takes executive action under delegated powers, to implement changes considered necessary to ensure a safe, secure and effective infrastructure.	6

(Continued)

Table 3.1 (Continued)

Activity	Details	Level
Communication	Responds to queries from clients/ users and contacts clients/ users (for whom the change management service is provided) to raise queries and provide information, entering details on to the client/user database where appropriate.	3, 4
	Provides advice to clients/users on the impact of requests for change and ensures that the appropriate impact analyses are carried out before changes are authorised.	5, 6
	Progresses status of changes with service departments to ensure that data is current.	4
	Reports to senior management on the progress and success or otherwise (i.e. failed changes) of the change management process, providing management information and statistics including performance against service level agreements.	6
Reporting	Interrogates the client/user database to produce reports for bodies that review changes, such as CABs, and for clients and management.	4, 5

(Continued)

Table 3.1 (Continued)

Activity	Details	Level
	Provides management information and statistics on the progress of changes to senior management and clients/users, including performance against service level agreements.	5
Review	Facilitates regular assessments, reviews and audits of the change management process, taking ownership of the findings and expediting action to close gaps.	5, 6

Taking each activity group in turn, the sections that follow dive into more detail about what is involved.

CHANGE MANAGEMENT PROCESS

The change management process drives all the activities of the change manager. The change manager owns, delivers, maintains, improves and promotes the process, making sure it is available for participants to access and that they know how to use it. As just one service management function of many, change management is unlikely to operate in isolation and the change manager works with other process owners to weave the inputs and outputs into a consistent whole that meets principles set at a higher level; for example, documentation and reporting requirements. Notable aspects of the change management process are described below.

Change management policy

Change management policy is the set of rules that governs the application of change management in an organisation. It determines what is and what is not subject to change management, so that those making changes can factor in the requirements of the process when they are planning their changes. Policy can include the roles and responsibilities of all stakeholders in the process, conformance expected and the consequences of deviation, accountability requirements, priorities, measures and so on. The policy sets out expectations for employees, contractors and third-party suppliers, who must be familiar with it.

According to SFIA**plus**, change management policy is set at the highest level of process seniority (shown in Table 3.1 as level 6). Although the change manager holds ultimate responsibility for publishing change management policy, it is unlikely that they would set it unilaterally. They should be able to provide good practice guidance, may propose a first draft and will probably make final decisions, but stakeholders should be expected to contribute their views and comment on proposals. This may lead to disagreements or appear to facilitate opt out or weakened change management, but it is more effective in the longer term to seek buy-in early and include everyone in a journey that will unfold rather than leave with a half-empty bus and expect them to catch up of their own accord.

Consult, test, revise. Repeat

Consultation is important if you are trying to implement a change management policy where it hasn't been done before, because the impact on participants will be significant. There is no point announcing that all changes will be subject to change management henceforth, if that brings the business to a grinding halt. It may be more palatable to start with a light touch, making only certain types of change subject to scrutiny; for example, those that may have caused problems in the past, or a specific project. This in effect is a process pilot and as the process is evaluated through the first attempt, it can be refined and expanded in later exercises.

Not only does this satisfy the business need to keep moving as unhindered as possible, but it includes everyone in defining the process from the start, giving them the chance to put forward their concerns and ideas before the process is finalised. It also has the advantage of introducing change management in short iterative cycles, which means that the benefits are realised more quickly than through interminable planning that results in revisions anyway. It is Agile by another name.

The bottom line is that no one person can expect to be able to speak for all viewpoints, and, understandably, people can be touchy if someone appears to assume that they can. The final policy must respect that and the change manager must invite contributions from all affected: in IT, in the business and from suppliers. To fail to do so will almost certainly result in resistance when the policy clashes with local practices that the change manager didn't and couldn't know about. Always ask first.

For more detailed guidance on what should be included in a change management policy, the ITIL® Service Transition publication[1] is a good place to start. **Chapter 4** contains some further tips on successful process implementation.

Process ownership

The change manager owns the change management process. This means accountability for the operation of the process, its health and its development. The buck stops at the change manager for all things change management.

If one doesn't exist already, the change manager will need to design and implement a change management process that supports the change management policy. This includes establishing lines of review and approval, evaluating tools, arranging procurement, managing implementation and

---

[1] https://www.tsoshop.co.uk/AXELOS-Global-Best-Practice/ITIL/#Service-Transition

configuration, and putting in place appropriate meetings and communications. They will write procedures in line with company standards and take responsibility for training participants. This could mean preparing and delivering training material themselves, or working with dedicated training staff, according to local custom.

Your process needs your training

Although generic change management courses and qualifications available commercially can provide a useful baseline of knowledge for all participants (see Appendix: References and Further Reading for some examples) an additional layer is still needed to convey local realisation according to the tools selected and configured to support the organisation's own change management policy.

Implementation is just the beginning; the change manager must maintain the process, and almost certainly improve it. Regular activities include the housekeeping and maintenance of software systems and databases; administration of user access and rights; the management of workflow through the process; and the management of changes to configuration of the change management tool. However, it is not a given that every change management process is supported by software tools designed for the job. They can be expensive, and it is possible to introduce the process using generic office productivity tools as a starting place from which the change manager can continually improve the process and its delivery.

The change manager is also responsible for ensuring conformance to the process. It is not enough to wield a stick and complain that it is ineffective. Cooperation is a two-way street. The best way to achieve this is to avoid looking like a dictatorship and take an inclusive approach from the start. Process owner doesn't mean 'do as I say' as much as 'do as we have agreed'. In the end, pragmatism may be required but as long as cooperation has been inclusively explored, the change manager is empowered to have the final say and management commitment to that should be unconditional.

Above all, the process owner must ensure that the process remains fit for purpose. It is a mistake to think that an agreed and implemented process is a finished one. As enthusiasm for identifying and mitigating risk increases, the risk is that the process becomes over-engineered and an over-engineered process is a waste of people's time. The nuances of change management allow for infinite refinement to ensure that changes go through the process as quickly as possible, with the minimum amount of impact on those involved.

Every time a change is made, lessons can be learned and these should contribute to improving similar changes next time around and improving the process when this is possible. As a result, the change management process should be in a constant state of flux. As regular changes begin to follow the same approaches it becomes absurd to expect participants to keep jumping through the same process hoops, but a copy-and-paste loses its value when it becomes lip-service only. The change manager, as process owner, must be vigilant to dilution of the process, but open to constant reinvention to reduce its footprint as much as possible. Fast-track and emergency changes are discussed in the next section.

Ownership means keeping the process alive and helping it mature; a stagnant process is not keeping pace with the overarching benefit of having it in the first place – continual improvement.

Process – regular, fast-track, emergency

The backbone of change management is a consistent process for defining, specifying, approving, building and implementing changes – everything that the change management policy says is subject to change management goes through the same process, no exceptions.

Apart from when it doesn't. As mentioned in the last section, when a change becomes routine the risks are reduced because the outcome can be predicted more reliably. An example is the regular implementation of the same change, such as a standard maintenance procedure. It is unnecessarily bureaucratic to make the people carrying out the same tasks under the same conditions write out the same change request every time they want to do it. But it is reckless to dismiss the process altogether. Traceability is an important aspect of change management. The middle ground is the change request that is based on a template, cutting out unnecessary rework and focusing only on the variable details such as dates, time, people and so on. The impact, risks and mitigation should be the same at their core, so redocumenting those should not be necessary, but they should be considered for their variables. Approval still takes place, which gives an opportunity to query assumptions, but can be fast-tracked with minimum discussion and maximum efficiency.

At the other extreme there is the emergency change. If something must be done quickly, to restore a critical business system to operation or resolve a security or safety issue, for example, the regular process should not be effective enough – it is not so much that the process is too slow for immediate changes but that the process doesn't need to be immediate for most of the throughput. Therefore, an emergency change process should exist to facilitate these types of changes by exception. Typically, an emergency change process involves going through the same establishment of facts, such as impact of the change, risks and mitigation, without necessarily formalising them into a written change request before the change is approved. To compensate, it requires the involvement of senior IT and business representatives to consider the risks and plan in real time, with supporting documentation prepared retrospectively when (as soon as) the immediate threat has been mitigated. Since there is an inherent risk in doing nothing, the risks of acting without the full process become part of the mitigation itself, but that shouldn't be at the expense of proper record-keeping. Events will still need to be reviewed after the fact, especially if the change fails, so the sooner it is written up the better. An emergency change should not be signed off as complete until the paperwork has caught up.

Use of an emergency change process can be controversial and the change manager may have to make a judgement as to whether something is a valid emergency, or something that is only inconvenienced by the regular process. Management commitment to supporting the change management process, and by association the change manager, is essential if rules are to be upheld and anarchy is to be avoided. The credibility of the process often hangs on abuse of the emergency change option by managerial escalation through operational IT and business departments seeking to avoid disruption to their own (lack of) planning. It is at times like these that management commitment shows its true colours. If the process is regularly undermined in this way, it can be very difficult to maintain the process at all.

Having said that, too many instances of people trying to take the emergency route could indicate that there is something wrong with the process that means it does not fit well with the life cycle of changes. Don't assume the process is faultless; taking a full textbook approach doesn't necessarily work for all situations and good practice is a moving target. A good change management process should be fit for all eventualities and work like clockwork in each, with a default process to manage new untried change; a fast-track process to push through well-rehearsed repeated change; and an emergency process to enable immediate threats to be mitigated effectively without throwing risk to the wind.

ITIL® Service Transition[2] provides comprehensive guidance on the details of developing change management processes.

Procedures

The change management process is the set of steps to be followed; procedures describe how this is done. As part of producing a change management process, the change manager must also produce procedures to explain what participants must do to make it work.

---

[2] www.tsoshop.co.uk/AXELOS-Global-Best-Practice/ITIL/#Service-Transition

Procedures (and processes) should be documented for reference. Documentation may be used as source material for the development of training material and it should be possible to use procedure documentation as a checklist against which to act, providing a working job-aid for those for whom it is not yet automatic. Training is never the one-off exercise that exists in a self-contained, ideal world. People take on new roles; they come and they go long after the initial implementation programme is complete. There is always a business-as-usual element in training, to deal with inevitable continual change. Procedures must be maintained in line with process change anyway, but training material, too, must reflect the latest process and be fit for purpose at whatever level – usable by IT and business staff, technicians and senior managers alike. Even in a large organisation with a dedicated learning and development function, as the process owner the change manager is accountable for making sure that training happens and is effective.

Documented procedures also contribute to the body of evidence of compliance with standards and legislation, so the requirement may be specified at a higher level in the organisation. It is common for procedures to follow a standard format using templates. An overarching IT service management function might be responsible for specifying the design of procedures, if not writing the text. The change manager may work with an administrator to fulfil the obligation, or they may be their own scribe. But produce procedures they must. They form the basis of how participants comply with the process and compliance should be audited against them.

It may be that change management software tools can be used to embed intuitive workflows that guide process users dynamically, but it is good practice to have a master reference document that represents the definitive configuration. You can use this as the basis for process changes; to identify unauthorised (re)configuration; to demonstrate compliance with standards implemented by the organisation; and to develop training material. It is also a good back-up for continuity purposes – if for some reason your change management system becomes unavailable for an unworkable length of time, you have something to refer to in the creation of a temporary workaround – if you don't already have one prepared as part of business or service continuity planning.

Simple rules for effective procedures

Keep it simple. Procedures should be pared down to unambiguous, easy to follow instructions – they are for reference, not bedtime reading.

Don't pad them out with unnecessary background or waffle to make them look more than they are. You want people to be able to go straight to the information they need. The harder it is to locate, the less likely they will be to comply correctly, because they will give up looking for the answer before they find it and guess what to do.

Include a flowchart with numbered steps. Number the instructions to relate to the flowchart steps. Put them on pages facing each other so they can be seen side by side.

Have someone unfamiliar with the procedures test them. When we write procedures for processes we already know well ourselves, it is easy to make assumptions and miss things out. However well you think you have written your procedures, always get someone less familiar to try them out.

Process engagement

Process engagement is a very important activity for the change manager. For reasons already stated, a change management process often represents a change in the way people work and promoting awareness of the importance of a structured change management process is a vital part of its success.

On a practical level this means encouraging people to participate willingly and constructively, not telling them what to do! If someone is engaged in a process it means they are actively participating and contributing to it, not having it done to them.

Process engagement activities range far and wide. It is unlikely that a change management process will exist on its own; to have got this far up the IT service management mountain almost certainly means that there will be at least a process for reporting faults to IT support. It may be that a suite of processes is being implemented over time or change management might just be the latest initiative. In a structured programme of change there should be an overall engagement approach, but, in any case, the change manager is responsible for change management process engagement.

Change management has inputs from and outputs to other processes, so engagement with other process owners is also important to make those links work effectively. Specifically, problem management could identify changes that will fix faults, so the problem manager will be a regular customer. Also, anything that records baseline information will need to be updated when changes are made, so this is a key output. Examples include a formal or informal configuration management system or database(s) and any derivative records, including network topology diagrams, system documentation and continuity plans. Change manager interfaces and dependencies are covered in detail in **Chapter 7**.

At a strategic level, process engagement could include working closely with prospective participants to design and implement the process, running training programmes and delivering awareness presentations. At a tactical level, how the change manager operates and engages with participants is part of the public relations function that holds the process together. Engagement is a continual requirement and a continual effort.

Change management can be perceived as a barrier to change and it is important to dispel preconceptions from the start.

Selling the benefits of change management, described in **Chapter 1**, is a necessary part of engagement. Don't assume that everyone understands it. Also make sure that the change management process is geared to ways of working in the parts of the organisation that are required to engage. A good example of this is in software development. There is no point having a change management process that is designed for a protracted waterfall software development methodology with monthly change review meetings if Agile methods are used and changes are expected to go in every week.

Process engagement amounts to buy-in and techniques for maximising it are explored in more detail in **Chapter 4**.

PROCESS OPERATION

Day-to-day change management process operation is the core activity of the change manager. It can be divided into three main areas: handling requests for change; facilitating the review and approval of requests for change; and maintaining the system.

Handling requests for change

The request for change is the mechanism for putting changes through the change management process and it is covered in detail in **Chapter 4**. Normally, a request for change is created by someone closely involved in the technical aspects of its planning, development and implementation because they are best placed to understand the impact of a change, and conveying the impact adequately is fundamental to getting it approved.

However, the change manager may assist in ensuring that adequate information is provided in requests for change. As the gatekeeper of changes on their way to review and approval, the change manager needs to make sure that reviewers have enough detail to make decisions based on impact on services; risks associated with making a change;

and plans for reversing a change if it fails, for example. To ensure this, the change manager may refer requests for change back to authors with guidance for required clarification if the information provided is perceived to be insufficient. This is not to obstruct the process, but to get it on track and reduce the likelihood that changes are held up later and cause even more work. As part of this, the change manager will consider the audience and make sure that the language used does not bar anyone from making an informed decision. For example, language that is too technical or too jargonistic could exclude business representatives. The first stage in the process for a new request for change, then, is acceptance by the change manager.

This can be simplified for all concerned by using standard templates for fast-track changes. When changes are repeated regularly, for example for standard maintenance activities, it makes no sense to write them out from scratch each time if the core activities, risks and impact remain the same and only variables need to be considered – like the suitability of the planned date for implementation. Standard templates save time for those creating requests for change who do not need to reinvent the wheel and for the change manager who does not need to go over old ground. In many ways, such changes that are standardised for fast-track are less risky than if they were rewritten each time, because rewriting means rethinking and, to use a popular phrase, if it is not broken don't try to fix it. The other side of that coin is that something forgotten once could be forgotten forever, but that's where the post-implementation review process can help; more on that later.

The change manager must be alert to the possibility of insidious scope-creep of fast-track changes. This is the temptation by change authors to attempt to rush through variations on a theme as repeat changes that are not, in fact, approved and legitimate for fast-track templates. Similar tactics include artificially lowering the impact and risk ratings and attempting to pass off a major change as a minor change. The change manager will validate that the correct category has been applied before allowing changes to be reviewed for approval, to ensure that they take the appropriate route.

Major and minor changes

Categorising changes as major or minor is a way of enabling appropriate progression. What is deemed to be major or minor is, of course, subjective and open to local interpretation, but it is a useful way to group changes for efficient processing; for example, changes that must be approved by a change advisory board (major) and changes that can be approved at a lower continuous level (minor).

Categorisation is also a useful tool for filtering records for measurement and reporting.

Perhaps the main justification there can be for directly involving the change manager in writing requests for change is the case of emergency changes. This may be the best way of getting an emergency change thought through and presented in a way that can be reviewed easily by those who will approve its implementation. In this case, the change manager takes on the role of scribe when probably everyone else involved is too busy being technical. Doing this absorbs the change manager review, as they must be able to understand the implications and the actions to be taken to be able to write the request for change in the first place. But this should be the exception rather than the rule, as should be the case with emergency changes. If the change manager gets into the habit of writing up every change, they risk making assumptions that are incorrect and slip back into the territory of marking their own homework as well. Part of the point of change management is review by others because collaboration provides a more robust solution and a better guarantee of success.

Facilitating review and approval

Once the change manager has rubber-stamped the quality of a new request for change in principle, they can release it for review as specified in the process. The route will vary, depending on the nature of the change. Peer review will involve people with similar skill sets casting an eye over each other's plans to provide constructive input – two heads are better than one. Hierarchical review will provide managerial and financial authorisation to proceed.

Review and approval exist at different stages in the life cycle of a change. In the first instance, a proposed change is considered for permission to spend time and money developing it. No change should get to the implementation stage without this having happened. Budget and line managers will typically make or break a change at this stage, and it should happen early enough so that it doesn't cause too much waste or disappointment! Once a change has been planned and made ready, it should be reviewed for quality of design; mitigation of risk; and preparedness for all eventualities, including backing out of an unsuccessful attempt at implementation and restoring the status quo without further disruption to business users or detriment to long-term service. All things being equal, it is approved and scheduled.

There will be many review and approval paths through IT departments, third-party suppliers and business departments, according to specialisms, departmental divisions and projects. A change might go through several stages of build, involving different people at different times. For example, an application upgrade might start life in software development and testing but be applied by server specialists responsible for the live operational environment. Sometimes a change might require a new path and the change manager will be responsible for advising and facilitating in this respect.

Review and approval depend on the circulation of written requests for change. The most efficient way to do this is using a change management workflow software system designed for the job, but it is feasible that a small-scale operation might use generic office productivity tools such as word processing and spreadsheets.

Sometimes it is enough to authorise changes in real time, as they do the rounds – usually if they are fast-tracked changes or relatively minor in risk and impact. For the rest, it is common for the change manager to host a regular change advisory board meeting. This is a bringing-together of those seeking approval for changes and those approving them, providing them with an opportunity to discuss plans and schedules, and iron out any wrinkles leading to approval, details of which are then recorded by the change manager (or their office), for traceability and evidence. The records of change advisory board meetings can form the basis of a rolling change schedule, providing a consolidated view of what is approved and when it will be implemented. This is usually shared with a wider audience, including business departments and service users who will be affected directly or indirectly by the changes.

The change advisory board and the change schedule are important for managing and communicating change. They appear again in the communication activities later in this chapter and are explored in practice in **Chapter 4**.

Maintaining the system

Setting up the change management system is part of process implementation, but, like training, it is unlikely to be a one-time only activity. New system users will need to have accounts set up; those leaving will need to have theirs decommissioned; access rights will be modified with role changes; and passwords (often frequently) reset.

Workflows may need to be reconfigured in the event of organisational restructuring, or new ones set up and old ones removed as projects start and finish.

Process review may result in modifications to the standard request for change template or review and approval routes. The acceptance of tried and tested repeat changes will result in the creation of new fast-track templates and automatic approvals.

Membership of the change advisory board might change when people change jobs; new names might be added to a rota to spread the load and the experience. It is not unusual for service desk analysts to take it in turn to represent the service desk for the board. This is to fit in with shift patterns but also to expose them to work in progress that they may be fielding questions about, or, in the worst case, dealing with incidents caused by a failed change (which of course we expect change management to avert).

Configuration management

Perhaps most important of all is the data about the components of change and the services they underpin. According to ITIL®, this is part of the remit of service asset and configuration management (SACM), which is a separate, but complementary, process because the data held is both an input to change management and an output from it.

In a fully functioning change management system, those creating requests for change should be able to identify the components and services involved in a change from data that already shows how it is currently configured within the IT estate. This informs understanding of the impact of a change on components and services and identifies the people affected. This is a crucial part of the change management process because it enables reviewers and approvers to base their decisions on shared and verified facts. If the data isn't available, impact assessments may, at best, be a guess, and at worst not known with any certainty at all.

Change and configuration management should ideally form a closed-loop process. The configuration data that is known forms the basis of change planning and is updated following successful change implementation, maintaining a solid base of reliable information on which to design the next change. The importance of having accurate configuration management data when planning changes, therefore, should be obvious, as should be the need to make sure that when changes are applied, the database is updated to reflect this or the next change risks being based on incorrect information. The configuration manager role might sit with someone other than the change manager, or the change manager might be responsible for that too.

Configuration management is not limited to physical pieces of hardware and software, it encompasses everything relating to a service. A comprehensive configuration management database (CMDB) or system (CMS) should therefore trigger a cascade of updates following a change, including system and user documentation, training materials and continuity plans, as well as altered components and the relationships between them.

The crucial relationship between the change manager and the configuration manager is explored further in **Chapter 7**.

The process for service asset and configuration management is covered in detail in the ITIL® publication Service Transition.[3]

Maintaining the system is unlikely to be a daily activity, but it must be factored into the workload so that pending administration does not obstruct the process from functioning as it should.

CHANGE IMPLEMENTATION

The change manager does not normally implement change but is closely involved in the steps that lead to it. The extent of their involvement is described in this section.

Change status

The change manager is ultimately responsible for ensuring that the status of a change is reflected in the change management system. This may be automated or require manual intervention, or it may be a combination of the two and may vary along a continuum according to the level and type of change. For example, a fast-tracked change may have fully automated approvals, while a major change will almost certainly require ratification at a change advisory board meeting before it can

---

[3] www.tsoshop.co.uk/AXELOS-Global-Best-Practice/ITIL/#Service-Transition

be moved to approved status. Status determines readiness for the next stage in the process, whether that is further approval, implementation, post-implementation review or closure.

The change manager will use status information to prepare agendas for change advisory board meetings, and to provide updates to interested parties on request. However, tracking the progress of changes through the review and approvals process should be carried out by those involved as a matter of course, who should have access to status information directly.

Although some approvals may be generated by approver action, others may need to be confirmed by the change manager; for example, in the case of major changes and emergency changes, but as dictated by local policy. This might also be true of changes that have been approved subject to further action being taken, which can be specified at change advisory board meetings to avoid deferring a change to the next meeting, calling an extra meeting or circulating updated information between meetings for ad hoc consideration. The change manager verifies that the additional activities are complete before updating the status, avoiding unnecessary disruption to plans and time wasted on more meetings and administration.

Whichever way it is done, the onus is always on the implementer to confirm status before executing a change. They should not need to depend on the personal intervention of the change manager to tell them they can proceed as this could easily become a bottleneck, building in process delays and interfering with the change manager's proper job, which includes making up-to-date status information available in real time for this purpose.

Another aspect of change status is tracking the progress of changes according to plan. It is as important for the change manager to know that plans are unchanged as it is for the change implementers to know that they may proceed, not least so that schedules can be kept up to date, but also because changes are approved as planned and a deviation can affect the decision to go ahead. Strictly speaking, a change that misses its slot must be reapproved for a new time, allowing potential clashes with other plans to be considered.

Change execution

As well as being kept to schedule, change execution (or implementation), must be done according to the details specified in the approved request for change. It defeats the purpose of the process to have a change assessed and approved based on one argument and then to deviate from that argument and do something different on the day.

The implementation of change is not usually carried out by the change manager, but they might feasibly be involved in the real-time exercise. For major changes with high impact, a change manager will usually expect to be informed of progress according to plan, or at least the outcome – whether they are successful or otherwise – so that they can be proactive in keeping stakeholders informed.

Executing emergency changes

The change manager provides a valuable service by protecting those actively involved in implementation from the many and varied others who may want to know how it is going. This is especially true in the case of an emergency change, when there might be pressure to fix something quickly in the uncertainty of the moment. This is a double hazard because often an emergency change means that those normally occupied by services now not working are free to roam in search of entertainment and perhaps the kudos of being associated with the war room.

Discouraging hangers-on

Never order more pizza than the core implementation team can eat, and never leave it in view of others.

Caveat: it is not good practice to have food in a data centre!

In the event of an emergency change, the change manager might expect to give the go-ahead for implementation to take place having metaphorically, or literally, walked the plan around senior approvers. In this situation it is a good idea to document the outline plan on the fly so that there is something to flesh out for the record later.

In the heat of an emergency, the change manager is a step away from the fire and can provide valuable support to those with the hose. The change manager should be in a good position to advise on the risks associated with an emergency change. They live and breathe the plans in the pipeline and will be better informed than most about potential clashes and synergies. They may need to prioritise an emergency change over other work; this might mean disrupting the immediate change schedule, or it might have a knock-on effect to changes in preparation that must be parked during the crisis.

The change manager can advise and update in both directions, adding value to the process for all parties. In the absence of some or all anticipated senior approvals, the change manager may be empowered to make the 'go' or 'no go' decision on their behalf.

Change manager reminder

Take your share of the pizza with you, or risk missing out.

Post-implementation review

At the most basic level a post-implementation review (PIR) must be carried out to know whether a change has been implemented successfully or not, however cursory that may be. A request for change cannot be closed until the outcome is known. Those involved in implementation should update the request for change with the outcome.

If a change fails or is only partially successful, the plan and the actuality should be reviewed so that lessons can be learned. The extent to which the change manager gets involved directly in this will depend on the nature of the change and local interpretation of the process.

For major and emergency changes that fail, the change manager should convene a post-implementation review meeting comprising representatives from all areas involved in the change and affected by the impact of the failure. In addition to the technical staff who planned and executed the change, this could include the business areas whose work may have been disrupted and certainly the service desk and problem management staff caught up in any fallout. The change manager should document the outcome and publish the findings. Post-implementation reviews for high-profile change failures are likely to have a far-reaching audience with a high level of seniority, and the change manager should expect to front the presentation of shortcomings, regardless of their source.

For minor changes, it may be that the change manager delegates the task to someone directly involved in the change. For those changes that aspire to become fast-track, this is not going to happen until the post-implementation review has come up with solutions to any incidents. Post-implementation reviews for relatively benign failures should still be recorded, and lessons learned should be filed where they will be found next time a similar change is planned. Ideally this will be against the record for the component that was subject to change, typically in the configuration management system or database. If the service asset and configuration management process is weak, the change manager is advised to make provision for recording and making available lessons learned as part of the change management toolset.

One way or another, the change manager needs assurance that post-implementation reviews take place and are recorded usefully. Validation of this should form part of their process monitoring activities, discussed in **Reporting** and **Review**, later in this chapter.

Change completion

Not to be confused with change execution, or change closure, change completion is the milestone mark at which change implementation is reported as finished. That is, the approved plan has been executed and the change has been implemented, or not, partially or fully. It cannot really be considered as complete until a post-implementation review has been done, which, in the case of successful change, is brief ('Was it successful? Yes.') and can lead straight to completion. In a devolved change management workflow system, it is usually up to the implementer of a change to update the system with the outcome and they should do this as soon possible after the event.

Unless the change manager is critical to maintaining the integrity of records, the only reason they should get involved in updating them to reflect change completion is if they are managing a change directly – such as an emergency change that they have recorded thus far – or if they have taken over the management of a post-implementation review following a major or emergency change failure.

The change manager may find themselves contemplating the completion of change records if they have been neglected and outcomes have not been recorded in a timely manner, but this should be avoided for the sake of the integrity of other processes such as configuration management. Failed or partially failed changes should be analysed for lessons learned soon after the fact – while there is something to remember – and change closure should not be held up artificially by delaying the trigger of completion. Unfortunately, the impetus to complete the process can be lost when a change has been implemented successfully and the next change beckons.

It is unacceptable for the process to have loose ends, where changes that have been carried out are left with inconclusive records. It is up to the change manager to devise incentives for change completion if this is a problem, but they should be proactive in reviewing status regularly and should not let a backlog get out of control. They will also decide how best to classify different degrees of success and failure in accordance with reporting requirements. Any delays in updating requests for change with key flags such as this will affect reports and distort conclusions.

Change closure

Fully reviewed and completed changes should be closed, to indicate that a change has traversed the process and no further action is required. The change manager should not expect to have to do this, unless they alone manage the data. However, they should want to verify compliance with the change management process. For the sake of expediency, they might mark a change as closed, following consultation with those responsible, but they must have confidence in the process and act if a problem persists.

COMMUNICATION

Communication, through the change manager is the glue that binds the change management process. The paradox of change management is that it requires people whose talents lie in making technical things happen to spend time writing about them in ways that people whose talents lie elsewhere can understand. Writing about technical things is not so important to the technical person who just wants to get on with the job, which is why they chose a career in IT. Sadly, reading about technical things is not that interesting to the people they are writing for either, which is why those individuals chose a career elsewhere. This leaves the potential for a communications chasm when the less than enthusiastic writer is confronted with a captive audience.

Enter the change manager. As previously mentioned, they are the bridge between the technical and the non-technical and a lot of their activity relates to communication across the process and the organisation, filling in the gaps and making ends meet. This section covers key aspects of communication in change management that the change manager will need to own.

Quality of requests for change

The request for change is the primary vehicle for change management and it is discussed in detail in **Chapter 4**.

The change manager is the gatekeeper of all requests for change, whether they are normal, one-off regular changes; repeatable fast-tracks; or emergencies, and they must be happy with the quality of the content at each stage before they pass them on. This will mean reading new and updated requests for change, raising queries with authors and suggesting where clarifications are necessary. Certainly, if the change manager doesn't understand what is being said there is no reason to assume that others will, so pleading ignorance is no defence.

Information is required on a range of topics, not just the technical steps to be performed. A request for change must articulate comprehensive information about the impact of making a change – on services in the long term and while the implementation is being carried out – and the associated risks. Meaning must be inferred accurately by all readers so that assumptions do not inadvertently increase risk. This information must be expressed clearly enough for a non-technical person to understand what they are agreeing to.

The change manager will be active in facilitating this and must put themselves in the position of all readers to ensure that one size fits all. They may be under time pressure to do this, because invariably the author expects instant progression of something that is already good enough and delays at this stage are perceived to be the fault of the process. It is not in the change manager's interests to set insurmountable hurdles and expect enthusiastic participation, and they are advised to coach a timely resubmission rather than reject out of hand, but in return for their investment they should be able to expect continual improvement of subsequent first attempts. In any case it is a false economy to let something through now, only to have it rejected later.

Writing

Requests for change are all about writing. Writing a request for change enables it to be shared efficiently across physical and time boundaries, in much the same way that an online blog can reach a wide audience simultaneously. Writing permits the thinking and planning to evolve and the proposition to be edited until it is ready. The alternative is a stream-of-consciousness chatter on loudspeaker, inescapable for those with other things to do and as useful as a child repeatedly saying, 'Are we nearly there yet?' on an eight-hour road trip.

But many people don't like writing, especially technical people. The paradox of writing is that you need to do it to get better at it. It is a skill, only learned through practice. Saying, 'I'm no good at writing' is true if you don't write. Unfortunately, writing goes with most territories and it is wise to accept this early. The change manager has the misfortune to substitute the schoolteacher in persisting with the quest of clarity of prose. Happily, there is help available. The importance of writing for the right audience is recognised when crossing boundaries between business and IT and BCS has published two targeted guides to help: *Business Writing for Technical People*[4] and *Technical Writing for Business People*[5] set an example in needing no further introduction.

Use them to help improve the quality of writing in requests for change and assure authors that, since practice makes perfect, practice is all you require.

---

4 www.bcs.org/books/businesswriting

5 www.bcs.org/books/technicalwriting

Change advisory board

The change manager should host a regular cycle of change advisory board meetings and take the lead in related communication. This will include scheduling meetings and inviting members to attend, advising those preparing changes of agenda deadlines, preparing and circulating agendas and supporting material, running the meetings from the agendas, facilitating agreements in the meetings, recording the decisions made and circulating the formal minutes to participants after the fact.

It is up to those participating in meetings to use the agenda and the requests for change to prepare for their contribution. However, as before, the change manager can win friends and influence people by going the extra mile to make the process as easy as possible. The agenda should be structured in such a way as to make it easy for participants to locate the changes they are involved in, since it is unlikely that every attendee will be interested in every change. There may be no need for them to wade through the minutiae of every plan, which they can skim read if they wish and deep-dive into when it is important to them. Organisation by department, for example, might be enough.

The minutes of the meetings should record a summary of any decision-making process that takes place, to avoid going over old ground later ('Why did we decide that?'). A summary of the work to be done, including timescales and the impact the work will have, should be presented separately in a change schedule. Publishing the outcome without the details will make it easier for those involved in implementation to extract the information they need, and this can double as a communication to the organisation.

Change schedule

Unless there are reasons for confidentiality, openness and transparency should be the default setting for the change manager. They should be ready to communicate about changes, proactively and reactively. Business and IT staff alike might ask for a progress report on any change in the pipeline, at any time. That might mean looking it up, but quite often the change manager has absorbed enough information to give a convincing immediate response, which is a good skill for someone who might like to be thought of as a key player.

An important proactive communication is the preparation and maintenance of a consolidated change schedule. This should be a timetable and summary of all forthcoming changes and should include information about services and user groups affected and what this means for access during the change. The change schedule should be kept up to date and made available to everyone. If reminders and alerts can be triggered, even better. Not only does the change schedule empower departments and individuals to make informed decisions about their own workload planning, but it gives them an opportunity to raise any concerns or justify any objections. The lone ranger might decide to work on Saturday to catch up with a backlog and can change their minds before they get there if they know that the tools they need will be unavailable. The overtime planned to prepare that contract for the new client might be important enough to cause a change to be rescheduled.

Change management pivots on communication and new information can change the status of a change in an instant. Not everyone knows everything at any one time, and business plans can be prepared in parallel with no expectation of a clash. A change that is postponed goes back into the pot, all bets off, status: no longer approved. The change manager is the conduit and they must be ready to tell those about to jump to stay put in time.

Change updates

Once a change is over the line, it is reasonable to assume that some people will want to know the outcome. Not everyone will care about every change but departments with a vested interest deserve an update, as do senior business and

IT managers, even if it is just to say that everything went as planned, money well spent, thank you and goodnight! In the spirit of making it easy for everyone, the change schedule is a helpful vehicle for adding updates and outcomes. Why invent another wheel when this one is good enough?

The service desk is an often-neglected interested party. A change doesn't necessarily have to fail at the time of implementation to cause faults after the fact. These faults will be reported to the service desk. It can save a lot of wasted time and loss of face if the service desk is in the loop. If someone calls and says that they are having a problem with something that has been subject to a change that was perceived to have been successful, consider which of the two responses below gives the best impression.

Service desk:		Service desk:
'Hi. I'm sorry to hear that no one in your department can use the XYZ system this morning. A change was made to it last night. It was completed successfully and tested OK after the change. I will report your findings and come back to you. It may be related, or it may be something else.'	**OR**	'Hi. I'm sorry to hear that no one in your department can use the XYZ system this morning. A change was made to it last night. I haven't had an update since then. I will report your findings and come back to you. It may be related.'

Remember that the service desk is the shop window of IT. Whatever impression they give, everyone in IT is implicated. Obviously, neither of the replies above is good when people can't access the systems they need but the change manager can help the service desk to sound like they are part of the team, which will reflect well on everyone. It should go without saying that the following scenario should never occur.

> *Service desk:*
>
> Hi. I'm sorry to hear that no one in your department can use the XYZ system this morning. I'm not aware of any changes being made. I will create an incident ticket for you.

Not only does the service desk look clueless (which they are if they have been excluded), but they will now waste time trying to identify the cause of a fault when the biggest clue they could have had was that a change was taking place.

Everything in between

The glue that binds, the oil that frees, sticking, unsticking, whichever metaphor fits the moment, the change manager holds the process together and keeps it moving from start to finish through communication. This is inevitable because, although two changes might be similar, and lessons learned in between, the circumstances are always different because time has elapsed and bedfellows have changed. Last week's application upgrade no longer sits comfortably with this week's client commitments or next weekend's redundancy test. As Heraclitus said, you can never step into the same river twice.

The change manager is the constant that is gathering the wisdom of progress and building the more mundane master calendar of change. The change manager will be asked questions about schedules: whether this late arrival can be squeezed on to the agenda for the next meeting; whether a change reversed yesterday constitutes a new emergency change today; whether the impact suggested makes it a major or minor change; or whether it can be sneaked through as a fast-track.

It goes with the territory of fast-paced technological evolution that factoring in the change management process is a constant challenge. And when this provides a ready-made excuse, it is a door half open to kick. Being the change manager can sometimes feel like being the dam that holds back a torrent, but no one would wish to face the flood if the dam broke.

Readiness for the change advisory board, readiness for implementation, teams juggling multiple changes and so on. means that the change manager must sometimes chase up on progress. They can let laggards fail at the next change advisory board at their peril, but someone, usually at a more senior level, will argue that approach is petty and irresponsible. It is a team effort; the change manager must play their part in getting things across the line.

Fights can break out, metaphorically speaking, when the tension between responsibilities in the process boils over. At times, the change manager might think they are spoon-feeding the change owner and the change owner might think the change process is over-engineered. The change manager must always be the grown-up because it is their process and they must make it work. And supporting others to be compliant in the first place is always easier than telling them they have done it wrong and fixing problems after they occur. You want to be able to report on an effective process, not one that people try to work around.

It's not all doom and gloom. **Chapter 4** includes some tips for getting cooperation proactively; think of it as servicing the car regularly as well as checking the oil.

PR

Public relations is an important aspect of the change manager role. Given the propensity for the change management process to be perceived as an obstacle of change by those who just want to get on with it, those who police it must work hard on its image. Expecting participants to just do it may seem reasonable but getting them to do it voluntarily because it helps is the target. That way, the chance of lip-service only is reduced, as those writing requests for change start to grasp the benefit of thinking through the implications of what they are doing, rather than just making sure that every field has some text.

In the long run, singing the praises of the successes and putting a positive spin on the failures (it could have been so much worse with no planning at all!) can raise the profile of a beneficial process that encourages changers to get the quality of their requests right first time and reduce reliance on the change manager to intervene. Remember, it is in everyone's interests to devote time and effort to preparation that prevents problems, rather than having to spend it in a high-profile situation fixing something that broke. But that is why the PR is important. By being so efficient and successful at implementing change, it all too easily goes unnoticed. 'I don't know why the IT department has to be so big', they say, 'I don't know what half of them do.' Don't ram it down people's throats, but make sure you curate some well-positioned anecdotes and bulletins to show how well it is working. Even the failures can show that the process has a silver lining.

Positive spin

Changes still fail, even with a robust change management process. The point is the reduction of risk. When reporting on a failed change, or any unplanned impact on services, make sure it is contextualised. It is not necessarily success or fail, one or the other; partial success or the ability to back out a change without detriment to users are positive outcomes. Don't say a change failed and was backed out, we will have another go later; say a change failed but the process of preparing it ensured that the status quo was restored without anyone noticing a problem; we will use what we have learned to develop a new version.

Proactive communication

It is difficult to overstate the importance of communication in the change manager role. Have a strategy for that which you can control. Schedule information updates, make information available centrally, put out regular bulletins, be on time with the meeting agenda and be consistent, as this will educate people to know where they can find what they want without pestering you. They probably won't mind pestering you, and have no incentive not to, but you will mind when everyone is doing it.

Time management – proactive vs reactive

Being proactive means pre-empting events that are beyond your control by bringing them within your control as far as possible. If you proactively tell someone that a change has been approved for implementation, for example, you are spending time on it, but on your terms. If they ask you for that information, you are spending time on it, but on their terms. The first example is you choosing how you spend your time; the second is you being interrupted while you were doing something else.

Being a change manager can be stressful. You are at the mercy of everyone else's workload and objectives and these can often clash in the middle, leaving you trying to please everyone except yourself. Do what you can to mitigate this. Plan your communications, train people to know what to expect from you, then deliver it. There will always be ad hoc requests for information, and you will have to react to them, but you can minimise the impact on your time by being as proactive as possible.

If you still need convincing, consider everyone in the organisation asking you individually every Friday afternoon whether there are any changes scheduled for the weekend; it is a disaster waiting to happen if you don't communicate proactively. In the long run, you will almost certainly do less work. Put it all out there on your terms and take Friday afternoon off (maybe, if all your weekend changes have been approved by lunchtime).

REPORTING

Talking about change management is one thing and it is very important. Good PR can help you to sell your process by putting some gloss where doubters can see it. Evidence to back it up is important too though, and the change manager will also need to understand where it is working and where it can be improved so they know where to target improvement initiatives. Reporting should raise questions to find answers that create actions, and further reporting should confirm improvement or otherwise – a continual process as suggested in Figure 3.1. Measuring and reporting should therefore be regular, cyclic activities for the change manager, and some approaches to that are discussed in this section.

Figure 3.1 Practical reporting examples for continual improvement

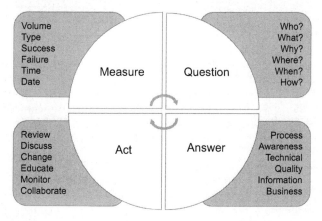

What to measure

Reporting can become time-consuming and complicated, especially if the data is not available in one place. It can be tempting to focus on measuring what can be measured easily and leave it at that. It can be tempting to say that something can't be measured because there isn't a button to press to churn out a report. If the tools are not available, it can be helpful to invest some time in taking some basic manual measurements (counting!) and presenting them graphically – to prove the process, but also to demonstrate the value that reporting can have and make the case for better tools.

It can also be tempting to measure too much, just because you can. Arguably, the most important recipient of reports is the change manager, so start with your priorities for measuring the state of the process. Don't waste time doing too much too soon. You must be able to act on the findings or there is no point in taking the trouble to produce them, so don't overload yourself with lots of data and no way to prioritise it or find time to use it. Do you really need to know more than one thing at a time? One statistic can generate multiple questions that can keep you busy for a while. Answer those before you ask for more.

There may or may not be value in knowing how many changes are processed over periods of time, but a baseline of basic information provides a starting place to measure trends. Is the number of changes going up or down? Is the proportion of emergency changes increasing? Why? The number of successful and failed changes is an easy measure with a high return. Failed changes almost certainly indicate that the change management process can be improved. Why did the changes fail? Was the impact identified correctly? Was the risk assessment realistic? Did the back-out succeed? If not, why not? Which part of the request for change was lacking? Was it peer reviewed? Was it approved by the right people? See how quickly the questions mount from simple facts!

Getting started

The advantage of taking very simple measures is that it is relatively straightforward to produce them, even with the most basic of tracking systems. If you don't have sophisticated process tools, you can easily build a spreadsheet that allows you to sort and filter key information. You might have to count rows and create charts and spend a bit of time manipulating the data, but in the absence of push-button reporting you will still get an insight into the workings of the process and be able to make improvements. Don't avoid reporting because you haven't got the tools; do what you can to make your case for them. If you can't demonstrate the value of your change management process, you can't move forward.

Reports provide questions, not answers

It is important to remember that measuring things gives you more questions, not answers. Of the question 'How many changes were processed last month?', an answer of, say, 25 or 125, is meaningless. The questions that arise from it are what make measurements useful. How does the number this month compare with the number last month? Who was responsible? What might it indicate? If the number has gone down, is that because there were genuinely fewer changes or because the process has been bypassed? How might you find that out? Why might the process be bypassed? If the number has gone up, was it because of failed changes the previous month or because there is more change coming through this month?

You must study the measurements and ask the questions to find the answers, but this approach will ensure that you focus your efforts on what you need to know, not on producing reports for the sake of it. Start by measuring what you can, if not what you'd like, but use what you find to inform the next question, and the next. Then balance what you'd like to know with the effort of finding it out. The value must exceed the effort and cost.

There are many possible measures that a change manager might want to take; this is a keep-it-simple starting place for you to build on, and a one-step-at-a-time approach to save you from wasting time and effort on things you can't use anyway. ITIL® Service Transition[5] provides a comprehensive list of suggested measures for further guidance when you are ready. See also COBIT®.[6]

---

5   www.tsoshop.co.uk/AXELOS-Global-Best-Practice/ITIL/#Service-Transition

6   www.isaca.org/cobit/pages/default.aspx

How to measure

One way or another, you will need to collect data about changes. Whether that is embedded in a dedicated change management process software tool or picked out of documents and sorted in a spreadsheet, or something in between, will depend on the maturity of the process and the resources at your disposal. **Chapter 4** provides more detailed coverage of what data overall you are likely to have in requests for change and **Chapter 5** discusses the tools available to support them. Feasibly, if you have the data somewhere you can report on it.

Starting from scratch, you need to make sure that what you want to measure is captured somewhere in the change management system, so define your reporting requirements first, if you can, to inform the classifications you choose. If you are introducing reporting to an existing system you will be constrained by what is captured already. As the process owner, you are empowered to configure the system to suit your needs but consider the impact of changing classifications on historical data (and on the people using the system – unannounced change is not a good example to set!).

When defining the data for your reporting requirements you should ask for the specific needs of others who may want reports from you. However, if they are unsure of their needs don't waste too much time up front on a wide range of data in the hope that it covers all eventualities. Concentrate instead on delivering what you know you need as soon as possible and share that first. Often, seeing something other than a blank sheet will prompt the right ideas to move forwards. As with many things, it is better to take an iterative approach than to spend a long time developing something based on vague ideas that miss the mark when they are finished. This is why Agile software development is so popular!

As requirements do emerge, keep them in mind for when you make configuration changes – classifications are your friend for the purposes of reporting.

Classifications

Classifications are groupings that you can specify to help you with measurements and reporting. They appear as filters in drop-down lists, also known as valid sets (of data). An example could be 'Normal', 'Fast-track' and 'Emergency' to give you a simple breakdown of the proportion of these types of change.

Classifications steer system users to select from choices you give them rather than letting them enter free-form text. Free-form text can produce variations on a theme and make your reporting difficult because you will have to consolidate meanings. Classifications take some effort, though, as they must be unambiguous if you are to steer users correctly, and if something is missing it can prevent users from entering data accurately in the first place. Finding the middle ground is important – too many classifications and it can become too difficult to find the right code for authors to bother making the effort, and errors creep in again.

As the process owner it is important that you have the final say on classifications and don't let a multitude of preferences across teams and departments cause overlap. A top-down view is important for consistent reporting.

What to do with your findings

The most important thing to remember is that the measures must be used for something. If they end up in a report that someone reads and files, they are of little value other than perhaps to show a volume of work. But even this doesn't prove that it is good work so it provides no justification for the process, or the role. If you are not asking questions and doing something with the answers, you are wasting your time measuring in the first place. (But not doing it is not the answer either!)

Continual improvement is the most reasonable expectation of any process. Start where you are and work out where to make changes to make it better a step at a time. Don't try and make it perfect **before** you start measuring, in the misguided hope of showing how good you are from the start. It is not realistic, and you will fail to demonstrate your progress and value. And in any case, where will you go from perfection? Your job is perceived to be done.

Examine the measurements you take and question the results. Compare reports over time to look for trends. Ask questions, review changes, test some theories, discuss findings and propose solutions (always involve others affected). Draw some conclusions to present to others, rather than expecting them to draw their own. Write an executive summary to go with your graphs. It is the change manager's job to interpret them. A simple example is shown in Figure 3.2.

Figure 3.2 Example of a simple report and commentary

Commentary

- Steady increase in maintenance changes (type normal).
- Throughput improved by creation of five fast-track templates for repeat work (week 3).
- Five changes from the transformation programme in week 4 kept levels up.
- Emergency change in week 2 should have been a normal change but timing of update from supplier missed approval at change advisory board. Exception made as business imperative to implement, but meeting arranged with supplier to discuss integration with normal process.
- Emergency change in week 4 as a result of failed maintenance fast-track. Fast-track status removed and change under review.

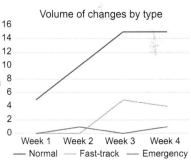

Volume of changes by type

Continual improvement can be applied to any aspect of change management depending on what you can measure in the first place. This could relate to the process steps; the quality of the information provided in change planning; the execution of change in a technical or timing sense; or anything else.

Never assume

Never take figures at face value. There is almost always more than one possible explanation. An increase in the number of changes doesn't necessarily mean that there are more changes; it might mean that that people were bypassing the process before and, fortuitously, changes went unnoticed (but unrecorded). From this you might conclude that the process has successfully won people over, or just that they have been told to comply. But don't guess – they don't necessarily mean the same thing for the future of the process, which must be fit for purpose not forced into compliance.

The difference between the statistics and their cause is the added-value the change manager must provide. Anything in between is just speculation, and speculation holds no sway outside its bubble.

The facts that underpin the reports you create are as many and varied as there are organisations and it is not possible to pre-empt them here. It is part of the change manager role to investigate the facts, using their knowledge of the local culture, the history of change management and the context of change management within other processes. When the change manager finds root causes, they can decide what must be done and this action is what matters, not the reports. Reports facilitate continual improvement; they are a means to an end, not an end in themselves.

Sampling

If it is too difficult to make even the simplest reports in order to kick-start continual improvement, you could carry out an occasional sampling exercise. Rather than collating data on all requests for change in a reporting period, instead focus on the details of one request for change. You can cherry-pick it – perhaps choose a major change that had a far-reaching impact, or an emergency change that succeeded or failed.

Look at the details you have. Consider in hindsight the information available. Look at the outcome. What could you have done differently? How long did it take to get it approved? Did you collect that information? Would it be useful to have that information in the future? They say that anything is easy in hindsight, but for it to be true you must look back. Reporting or no reporting, every little helps you inch forward in continual improvement, rather than endlessly repeating the same mistakes without even knowing.

Sharing reports

Possibly the change manager is the individual most interested in reports about change management performance because they are responsible for the process and have the greatest interest in where it can be improved. However, the information gathered can be of interest and use to others.

Line management
The change manager's line manager may want to see some evidence of an efficient and effective process and some demonstration of improvement over time. Acting on findings should show changes in the data. The change manager can say what they were trying to achieve, and reports should show whether they achieved it or not. There is no failure, only adjustment and going again. Nothing is guaranteed; only the failure to try is unacceptable.

Other managers
Departmental line and senior managers might also expect to see something that conveys return on investment (ROI). This is notoriously difficult to do, because for it to be accurate you must quantify the cost of the process and offset it against

the savings made by things that didn't happen, an exercise in 'what if' that has no real quantities to use. However, it is surely possible to model something to calculate the cost of the process, including overheads of dedicated staff and the time taken from other participants' 'real' jobs (of which this is a real part in fact). You might even come up with a hypothesis of net savings based on the success and failure of the actual changes that have taken place. But the effort required to place a monetary figure on the benefits of change management might outweigh the cost.

Realistically, calculating return on investment is a collaborative task. The change manager can collate the figures, but the figures need to come from all parts of the business, so there needs to be some consensus and willingness to cooperate in a process that has agreed value. The change manager can calculate the cost of the process from their own perspective, but the cost of service downtime needs input from service owners in the business. How much time technical staff spend preparing requests for change will vary and their own line manager is best placed to analyse that.

What I am trying to say here is that the ones who hold the purse strings may point to the change manager and say: 'prove the value of this process', but it needs organisation-wide commitment to pull the information needed together, so it must be driven from the top down and across the board.

Return on investment – using the process

If it becomes necessary to try and calculate ROI, and there is commitment across the organisation to provide the information to do this, you could use the process to facilitate gathering cost information as part of the impact assessment of a change – ask the question: If the change causes unplanned downtime, how much would it cost you, an hour or a day in productivity?

> Over time, you could build a picture of the value of
> services and use the outcome of changes, successful
> or failed, to demonstrate hypothetical cost. But it would
> be hypothetical since there is nothing to say that an
> unmanaged change would fail. You can't measure
> intangible things that might not have happened! You can
> only try and make a guess and if you spend more time
> guessing than managing the process, it is probably not
> worth it.

Whether you make some attempt at ROI reporting or not, you
can support it by keeping up the PR – mentioned earlier in the
communication activities. Every time a high-profile change is
a success, the PR machine should whirr into action. Ultimately,
that and strong evidence of continual improvement are more
practical and pragmatic approaches than formal calculation
of return. After all, change management has been around for
a long time, so its value generically should not need proof.
What is important is that your change management process
is fit for purpose in context and is the best it can be – no more,
no less.

Peers
Technical staff, teams and managers might want to see some
statistics from change management as evidence of their own
productivity. They might want to analyse their performance
to look for ways to improve how they do things too, but the
change manager will have an eye on that for them. The next
section is about review and you won't be doing that in isolation.
You should be working with others to identify ways to improve
the process collectively and you will initiate that process, so it
is not essential that others are proactive about this.

Business representatives
Business managers might want to keep an eye on what IT
has been up to on its behalf. In a large organisation that has
service level managers or relationship managers, or both,
it might be more appropriate to share reports with them.

They will be interested in successes and failures, and especially the impact on service availability, so if a change caused an unplanned outage, they might want the data on that to formulate their own questions. This might happen in real time, straight after such an event, in which case your reports would be used to underpin a post-implementation review. Indeed, you should initiate a post-implementation review to ensure that lessons are learned. More on those in **Chapter 4**. In any case, a service level manager will want to account for breaches of service level agreements represented by accidental downtime or show that accidental downtime was still inside a maintenance window, which might be the case! (And sharing that fact is good PR.)

Outsourced services
Possibly some, or all, of your IT services are delivered by a third-party supplier. If you have a fully managed service you might have contracted out your change management as well, which means you are probably reading this for fun (thank you). If you have a combination of internally managed IT and external service provision, you might think that change management responsibility should be split, with the supplier managing the changes they make. They should have a change management process and a change manager role, but they should work with you to comply with your process as well, once the change enters your space.

Outsourcing services can be a minefield and it is too easy to lose control of that which you paid for. You may like to share reports on changes made (only) by such service providers directly, and always with the service owner in your own company. You should expect them to reciprocate but you would be wise to make your own measurements of their performance anyway, or you risk your negotiating position. The service owner and anyone else involved in contracts with third parties will be glad of your validation.

Projects and programmes
Last, but not least, if changes are part of a bigger transformation project, you may be expected to produce regular information

to the other types of change managers up the hierarchy of organisational change. This might go into their overarching reports on an individual project or wider programme.

As the change manager is pivotal, it is reasonable to expect that anyone could request process performance reports. It is also reasonable to assume that they might not want everything, so you should expect to tailor reporting to individual needs.

REVIEW

Review is a natural extension of measurement and reporting. As already stated, there is not much point in producing reports unless you do something with the information in them, and this should be the basis for an ongoing process of reflection and continual improvement. In addition to reviewing and acting on reports, you should look for opportunities to speed up the process for as many instances as possible by reviewing changes for fast-track opportunities, not forgetting, either, to make sure that the findings of post-implementation reviews are fed into improvement. It is worth taking a periodic overview of these to look for trends. These and other specific interventions discussed below should consolidate and formalise your review strategy.

Change review for standardisation (fast-track)

The change manager should regularly consider promoting tried-and-tested repeat changes to standard fast-track changes that have a reduced or automatic approval process. Change requesters do not usually need encouragement to ask for fast-track changes to be signed off, but the change manager should nevertheless be proactive in stripping away the hurdles to change implementation. Don't worry, you won't run out of work.

Try to do yourself out of a job

Automate as much as you can with the aim of eliminating the change management process altogether. This will enable you to focus on progress and being ready to take on new requirements when the time comes, and your business-as-usual operation will be as lean as it can be. A win–win.

The change manager can advise on strategies to make the case for fast-tracking a change over and above the obvious evidence of past success, such as repeatable or automated testing, and thorough implementation and fall-back plans, as well as ensuring that such changes are always scheduled to take place in maintenance windows already established in service level agreements.

Standard vs fast-track

ITIL® calls pre-approved fast-track changes 'standard changes'. 'Standard' suggests that change-management-lite is the default position; fast-track suggests an exception to the rule. How you call it should reflect local change management maturity. Don't call it standard if deviation from the full process must be stated explicitly - it might prompt unauthorised change through misunderstanding. Don't call it fast-track if the project manager or scrum master already owns it.

Review of post-implementation reviews

Post-implementation reviews carried out after failed changes, especially those causing an unplanned outage or major incident, will provide the most valuable information about the quality of planning and preparation, and the change manager should take the lead in making sure that these happen as soon as possible after the event, while experience is still fresh.

It is important for the change manager to stay on top of the throughput of change and make sure that requests for change reach the closure stage. The imperative for a request for change is inevitably the need to do something and once that imperative has passed, the incentive to complete the paperwork has gone. In a large environment with a high volume of change it can be easy to lose sight of requests that have been approved for implementation, especially where post-implementation review is delegated. It can be a good idea to require formal update of the outcome and closure of all changes at the change advisory board, keeping them on the agenda until records are complete.

Managing change completion

You could use the change schedule as a vehicle for ensuring that positive updates are given following change implementation. Keep it as a standing agenda item at the start of each change advisory board meeting so that an update is required to formally remove changes from the schedule.

It might also be useful to develop a way to examine the status of requests for change in conjunction with the implementation date as part of the measurement and reporting activities. A simple list of changes where the post-implementation review status is still active, with the associated implementation date, will reveal the extent of the completion problem if there is one. Anything with an incomplete post-implementation review more than a couple of days after implementation is in danger of losing its imperative. The longer it goes on, the less accurate and detailed will the recorded outcome be because the facts will be forgotten (or the job will become too onerous).

Those implementing change tend to focus only on the hoops they must jump through to get their change approved for implementation. What happens after that is less important to them but is important to the change manager, who must have a realistic picture of the effectiveness of the process. If change records languish as implemented but open with no post-implementation review and no hope therefore of achieving closure, the change manager won't know how well the planning and approval process is working to effect successful change. If they are incomplete, they are left out of any reports measuring success or failure, a potential iceberg below the surface. Worse than that, incomplete change records might indicate that the CMS is out of date which will affect the planning of new changes. On the other hand, taking a good look at successful and failed changes with the benefit of hindsight will help to improve the process and the chances of successful change through lessons learned.

Even if the rate of success appears high and there have been no major-impact change failures it is informative to sample closed changes, either randomly or by cherry-picking, to consider the quality of the post-implementation review. It is too easy to just say 'done' and leave it at that, which reduces the process to a tick-in-the-box exercise with limited value.

Education, education, education

It is rarely enough to set some rules, train everyone and expect compliance to happen. Process failures often happen because of the failure to have a 'police' presence. If participants think no one is looking, they might be less than scrupulous; it feeds their 'what's the point?' bias. And they are right. If you don't look at what they write, what is the point of them writing it?

Requests for change must be looked at to get approved, so it's not so big an issue there. Make a habit of reading the post-implementation review and closure statements, but most importantly ask questions; let it be known that you have read them. Maintaining a police presence is part of the education process. Show the participants in the process that you are paying attention and that they are not wasting their time. You will learn something too, and that's the point.

Process audit

Formal certifications, such as those representing compliance with international standards (those prefixed ISO), require formal audits. Usually they take place annually in the form of a blend of internal audits – carried out by an organisation's own staff – and external audits – carried out by qualified auditors supplied by the certification awarding body.

Depending on the certification it may be acceptable for a change manager to carry out an internal audit of their own process, or it may be that this must be done independently by a peer or compliance representative, for example. Some organisations have a separate compliance team for this purpose.

Whichever way it is done, the change manager will need to cooperate with the audit and certification process and be trained in its requirements, probably as a condition of certification. Whether or not they are involved in internal audits, the change manager may be required to represent the process to external auditors. This will involve being asked questions about the process and evidence of its use, including demonstrating tools and providing records for examination.

When this is the case, the change manager role should have been involved in the preparation for initial certification to make sure that the process was fit for this purpose in the first place, but a new change manager may inherit the responsibility and it is important that they are familiar enough with the process to own it in front of an auditor.

Findings from formal audits will contribute to continual improvement, which forms the basis of standards' quality management. The change manager should be maintaining their own continual improvement system in any case.

There are a range of standards that include change management, and they are examined in **Chapter 6**.

Process compliance

Ensuring process compliance is an ongoing and strategic activity. Breaches of process, such as changes implemented without approval, may become apparent in the natural course of events. Change failures often have noticeable impact and unauthorised change might be traced from unplanned downtime. At a micro-level, detecting process breaches in real time will yield opportunities to restate, retrain, and examine the process for leaks and closures.

Auditing at a macro-level as a periodic strategic activity should unearth the ones that got away. Generally, the only way to do this is to compare the current IT service estate with a baseline and look for unauthorised changes as discrepancies between the two.

The easiest way for the change manager to achieve this is to work with the configuration manager, if there is one. Verification of configuration management system records as accurately reflecting reality is part of the configuration manager's remit. A by-product of that is a list of change management process breaches. Job done. If the change manager is also the configuration manager, they can consider the task as an overlap: two for the price of one.

If configuration management is less than mature, this can be more difficult. On one level, if individual teams have their own records of configuration items, which they should if they are able to manage what they are responsible for, the change manager can work with them to share baseline information and audit the estate in comparison. The drawback with that approach is that, in effect, it means these operational departments are marking their own homework, and depending on the reasons for breach of process, they may or may not have something to hide. It is not ideal for the change manager to be less than independent in this way, since it weakens their position and they can be easily undermined. As said previously, it is not a given that everyone wants to bypass change management and will if they can, but it does happen, and it is very difficult to demonstrate verified compliance to an auditor if controls are handed over in this way.

Another way to monitor unauthorised change is to use network discovery tools to take a regular snapshot of devices found and review exceptions between them. This reintroduces the impartiality of proper configuration management without maintaining configuration records daily. Updating configuration records with details of change, including outcomes and lessons learned, provides an audit trail that leads effect directly to cause. This saves time for the change manager and those planning new changes, and generally is the more robust vehicle for risk management. Taking a snapshot and playing catch-up periodically could be a good pragmatic solution between having everything and having nothing.

One step at a time

Implementing configuration management is not an overnight job. In order to succeed, it needs a good change management process to deliver its approved updates. Its benefits are many and varied, and outside the scope of this book, but suffice to say it is unlikely to be worth implementing just to demonstrate change management compliance. Simply gathering the baseline information can be a huge task, which often overlaps with live change while it is being carried out.

If you need a way to measure change management process compliance, you could try monitoring using discovery tools in the first instance to get an idea of how big, small or non-existent the problem is. If you find that the changes you detect are mostly supported by requests for change, and you are not experiencing implementation problems caused by planning against incorrect configuration item information, the cost of formal centralised configuration management might outweigh the benefits. If, on the other hand, you find that change planning is chaotic because there are no configuration records to plan against, and there is evidence of a lot of changes being made outside the process according to discovery tool snapshots, you have a case for introducing configuration management.

To break this task down into manageable chunks, a federated system might be the way to go – teams responsible for different parts of the estate gather and maintain their own records so they have something to plan against. However, these are linked conceptually to form a virtual central system and perhaps migrated to a physical central system a bit at a time, using the change management process. In the meantime, independent auditing of change management compliance can continue, using discovery tools.

Although not the subject of this book, configuration management does play a large role in effective change management. Service asset and configuration management is covered in detail in ITIL® Service Transition.[7]

Auditing the change management process for compliance can be a good way of kick-starting continual improvement. Records of breaches found, and the actions taken to prevent them from recurring, are ideal examples of issue management often looked for by certification auditors. Findings can also be used to inform independent process reviews.

---

[7] www.tsoshop.co.uk/AXELOS-Global-Best-Practice/ITIL/#Service-Transition

Process review

Regardless of all other interventions, the change manager should formally review the process periodically to make sure that everything is looked at, not just individual changes and post-implementation reviews, although relevant process-level findings discovered here should be fed into this overarching exercise.

It may be that there is a wider service management strategy to review all processes formally at specific times. This might be the case especially if certification audits are anticipated and would probably be scheduled to take place at an appropriate stage in the audit life cycle. For example, evidence of management reviews are a specific requirement of ISO 9001 certification and surveillance audits and are usually carried out immediately prior to an audit taking place.

In the absence of direction from a higher level of management, formal process review should be initiated by the change manager annually. Participants should include stakeholder representatives, including those who use the process to enable change, and those who benefit from the change enabled. The owners of other processes that touch change management should also be invited to contribute. More on who they might be can be found in **Chapter 7**.

AND THE CYCLE BEGINS AGAIN

It is important to remember that change means change, so the default position on the process should always be 'How must we adapt to meet new requirements?', not 'The process is finished; new requirements not accepted here'. The change manager is always standing on shifting sands and, as the embodiment of change, should convey the futility of resistance and set an example of continual improvement. Always have an open door and a standing invitation to all-comers to offer suggestions and improvements – but don't wait to be told what to do, keep moving.

Stay on top of good practice by reviewing the latest best practice. Know what is possible for process automation. **Chapter 5** discusses tools and what you should look for, but this is changing all the time. Make sure your sales representative tells you about new features for every major release. But read reviews and take part in user groups. Inform yourself independently in order to avoid being led into upgrades just because the supplier wants to make a sale. Apply your knowledge to your process reviews and invoke solutions that you need; don't just buy the latest functionality because you can.

Every improvement you make should be reflected in revised policies, processes and procedures, and that takes you back to the start. Figure 3.3 shows the activities outlined in this chapter as a continual cycle.

Figure 3.3 Change manager activities as continual improvement

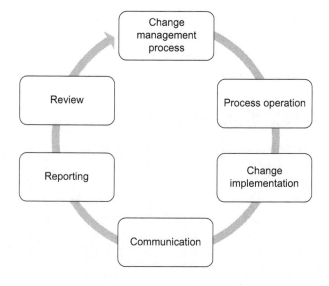

This is continual improvement in action, and it should be unstoppable – not because your process is never good enough, but because things are constantly changing, everywhere, but fundamentally in change management.

KEY POINTS

- The activities of a change manager are broad and varied.
- A change manager needs to be comfortable managing administration as well as being involved in technical work.
- Change manager activities should drive continual improvement of the process and the success of change.

4   METHODS AND TECHNIQUES

Chapter 3 discussed the activities of a change manager and at times alluded to how these are performed. This chapter goes into more detail about the methods and techniques that are at the disposal of the change manager, including the more prescriptive methods of operating the change management process, such as requests for change and the change advisory board. It also offers some softer, more subjective approaches to achieving objectives that are hard won through experience.

REQUEST FOR CHANGE

A request for change, often abbreviated to RFC, is the primary vehicle in the change management process. When a change is identified, the person responsible, usually someone in the IT team who will prepare it, creates a unique request for change. Initial information is expanded throughout the life cycle of the change – from initiation to final closure. At key stages, it is reviewed and approved, returned for more work or rejected outright, and it forms the history of the change.

The change manager receives new requests for change as the first point of contact in the process. They will either process them unchanged or refer to the author for more information. The change manager is the gatekeeper of requests for change and must consider the expected response of approvers before letting them through for review.

Add value

As the change manager, if you don't understand something written in a request for change others probably won't either. Don't pass things on with the assumption that reviewers or approvers will understand – ask for more clarification. It may be that you can't add value to a perfectly clear request for change, but if it is rejected later in the process because it is not clear enough for approvers, the process is failing and the change manager has not added value when they should.

The change manager is not normally expected to write requests for change, but they do need to be able to help authors understand what is required if they are falling short.

This section will explore the main parts of a request for change, the types of information required and their sources. It is a comprehensive list of the data and details normally required to enable review and approval – a summary is shown in Figure 4.1.

Although a request for change is usually a single artefact, the topics are a checklist and it may be acceptable for authors to refer to other sources rather than duplicate content, provided everyone who needs to see it can do so without undue extra effort. Content can be copied from elsewhere; for example, risk assessment information from project plans.

Essentially, the request for change is a document but it is presented as a computerised workflow in tools designed to enact the change management process. This makes it easier to manage multiple stages of review and approval. Tools are discussed in **Chapter 5**. The sections that follow expand on the content expected in a request for change.

Figure 4.1 Summary contents of a request for change

Metadata	Change details	Review, approval and implementation
• Unique identifier • Date created • Type (e.g. emergency) • Category (e.g. major) • Priority (e.g. 1) • Implementation date and time • CAB date • Completion date • Closure date • Other references • Author name • Author contact details • Business contact • Implementation lead • Other contacts • Approval status • RFC status (e.g. open)	• Description of change • Reason for change • Items subject to change • Impact assessment • Risk assessment • Test plan 1 • Implementation plan • Test plan 2 • Contingency plan • Scale and risk • Priority	• Peer review • Approvals • Implementation outcome • Post-implementation review • Completion and closure

Metadata

The metadata of a request for change is the product of key fields used for reporting purposes. Ideally choices are made from a valid set of options, to prevent illegal classifications that will make reporting difficult. This could be achieved by using a dedicated change management system designed for the process, or using a form created by spreadsheet software, for example.

As key fields, all these represent traceability, searchability and reporting on what can amount to a lot of data to be managed. Some might be updated as the request for change progresses through the process; for example, dates of meetings and implementation.

Unique identifier
Each request for change is unique and requires a unique identifier so that it can be tracked and found. This might be generated automatically by the change management system, assigned by the change manager or pulled from a predefined list. It is common to use a combination of letters and numbers; for example, RFC000001.

Dates

Date created, implementation date and time, change advisory board meeting date, completion date and date closed help to filter and sort requests for change for a variety of uses, including meeting agendas, change schedules and reports.

Other classifications

Type of change (standard, fast-track, emergency), category of change (major, minor), priority of change (1, 2, 3, etc.) and approval status can also be used to filter and sort requests.

Other references that link a request for change to its source and related work might also be included in a way that allows them to be used as key fields; for example, project references, problem references and unique identifiers of configuration items affected.

Names and contact information

The name and contact details of the person creating the request for change are essential as the primary contact throughout the life cycle of the change, but it is also useful to identify other relevant parties including the business originator of the change and individuals involved in implementation. The person creating the request for change should provide this information.

The names of approvers will also be required. They might vary depending on the level of the change and could be added automatically by a pre-configured system according to choices made (such as type, category and priority), or added later by the change manager. Also added later are approval decisions. Depending on the type and category of change, there may be one or more decisions at different stages of development.

Change details

Description of change

It should be obvious that a request for change should describe the change. This should be a narrative summary; explicit details of the parts involved and the plan to make the change are required elsewhere in the request.

Reason for change

Change for the sake of change is not a good business case. There must be a reason or cause for it. It might be to patch a security vulnerability, fix a problem or introduce new features. It might be preventative maintenance or housekeeping. It might be a new service requested by a business area, or it might be part of a bigger transformation project or programme.

To challenge the status quo there must be a benefit in making the change and a risk in not making it. Both should be included.

Example reason for change

The operating system patch will close a security vulnerability. If the change isn't made, the server and its services are exposed to potential malicious attack.

The change manager should consider the statement in the context of the rest of the request for change and ask for more information where this will help validate not just the change, but also its importance and urgency. A security patch on a server that supports the Human Resources system will be more important and urgent than a security patch on a development server that is not deployed in the operational environment (although the development team might say otherwise!). However, importance and urgency are also relative to other changes planned so the development server might take priority in a different context.

Perspective

Every change requester thinks their change is the most important and urgent, because it is their work and their perspective. It is quite common, therefore, for change requesters to make assumptions by omission – they don't need to explain the benefits of the change or the implications of not applying it; it is obvious to them. But the change manager must recast every change in the context of the bigger picture and needs the detail to be able to advise on this. It is not a question of undermining individuals or teams, but a question of overall business priority.

It is worth explaining this when asking for more information. People are more likely to comply and be more forthcoming next time if they understand the reason for the request and don't feel challenged.

Items to be changed
Details of all items affected by the change, and how they are affected, should be specified. It is not enough to just list the items that will have a change applied; the thing that is applied must be listed too. This is to make clear to reviewers, approvers and implementers explicitly what is going to change. It can also be used to verify configuration item records – if they are used to plan the change without a physical check on reality, it can be a useful check at the time of implementation.

Example items to be changed

Server 1: operating system ABC, version 1.23, updated with patch 4.56.

Server 2: operating system ABC, version 1.23, updated with patch 4.56.

This information may be recorded as part of the impact assessment or implementation plan.

Impact assessment
Getting a useful impact assessment can be troublesome, as it can sometimes be confused with reason for change. Reason

for change is the 'Why?' something is being done, whereas impact assessment is more about 'What does it mean?'

The impact of making the change should include the resources required, the cost, the return on investment if possible, the estimated time involved and the unavailability of services while the change is taking place. Identification of these services is important, because it will be necessary to get approval from those affected and make sure they understand the impact on their work and commitments of any downtime required. If you don't know what services are affected, you don't know who to ask. If service users don't know that services will be unavailable, they may be planning crucial work that clashes with the change. If there are service level agreements they should indicate pre-agreed maintenance windows, but it is not always reasonable to assume that they are there for the taking without notice.

Impact assessments must indicate which configuration item records must be updated following successful implementation. This will depend on what information is stored and at what level. For example, if you only record server configuration items with two attributes – memory and central processing unit (CPU) – you won't be able to update the server configuration item records with the new operating system version. But if the operating system is an attribute of the server in the configuration item record, this must be updated following successful change (or not, in the event of failure). The impact assessment provides the instructions for the things that must be done because the change has taken place, as opposed to the instructions for making the change itself.

This also applies to more peripheral objects such as documentation, continuity plans and training material. If you are upgrading an application to introduce new features, end-users will need to be trained in their use. This might have been arranged as part of a wider project but should be flagged as part of the change so that there is a complete picture of the impact and a check that everything has been done.

Impact assessment should also include negative impact if there is one; for example, what does it mean if we use these resources for this change? Does that have an impact on something else? Will another project or piece of work suffer as a result?

Configuration items

Configuration items (CIs) belong to the service asset and configuration management process in ITIL®. The configuration manager will be responsible for identifying the level of configuration items and this will depend on local interpretation of need for recording information about the IT estate and the things that support it. The range might include all hardware and software types, network components, process and procedure documents, end-user equipment, peripherals and so on.

Each CI type will have a set of attributes that can be a long or a short list of information associated with it. The decision-making factor is how easy or difficult it will be to keep it up to date. The more information that is recorded, the more time it takes to maintain it. Only record that which is useful to know; don't waste time capturing and managing information that is no use.

Although configuration items and the configuration management system or database are technically outside the scope of change management, they form a useful appendage. Changes can be effectively planned against an up-to-date configuration management system and the configuration management system can be kept up to date by effective change management (see Figure 4.2). The symbiosis is clear, and successful implementation of configuration management depends to a large extent on change management.

See ITIL® Service Transition[1] for a full description of
service asset and configuration management.

**Figure 4.2 The relationship between the configuration
management system and request for change (change
management process)**

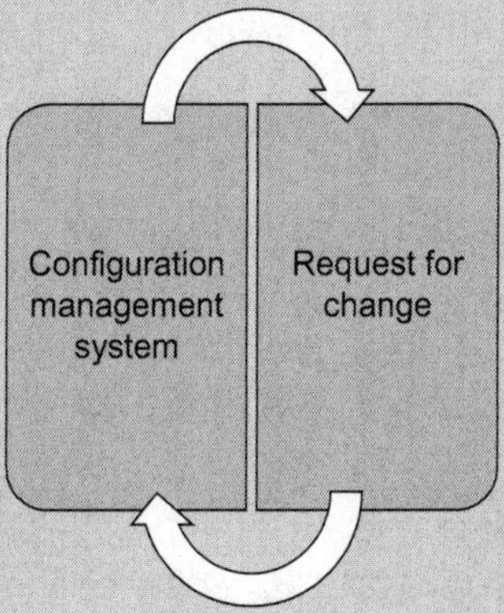

Risk assessment

The risks associated with a change must be identified, and
mitigated, as far as possible. This means that for every risk
there should be corresponding steps that will be, or have been,
taken to guard against them or limit the impact should they
be realised.

There are risks associated with making technical changes
that relate to the changes themselves; for example, how
mature a new service is, how tried and tested the technology
is, or otherwise. There are also risks associated with making
technical changes that relate to the business; for example,

---

1   www.tsoshop.co.uk/AXELOS-Global-Best-Practice/ITIL/#Service-Transition

readiness of end-users, or delays that make the risk of not making the change unacceptable.

Example risk and mitigation	
Risk	**Mitigation**
Loss of functionality	Back out and restore; make sure access to back-ups or original media is available in the change period.
New functionality is not understood	A comprehensive user training plan has been agreed and scheduled to take place the week before the change.
New legislation demands the change	The change is planned for implementation before the deadline.

Usually, a request for change is written by a technical person who will oversee the change or implement it themselves. Often, it is delegated to the most technical person involved because it is perceived to be a wholly technical document. However, this risks the risk assessment being from a technical-only perspective.

The author should involve the right people – in IT and across the business – to make sure that risks – in making the change and in not making it – are understood from all perspectives, and the change manager should make sure that this is reflected comprehensively in the request for change.

It can be a tricky area because the author may not know everything if the risk assessment for the request for change is left until later in the process, and in the interests of completing paperwork formalities there is the temptation to gloss over this with a narrow focus and pass it on to the change manager, rather than examine the change comprehensively in conjunction with other contributors to describe a balanced view.

Understandably, technical people are more comfortable assessing their own technical risks and perhaps do not expect to have to assess them from a business perspective – they are just doing their job as instructed. But the request for change still must present the full picture and the author should be able to request input at least from the business source of the change, a business analyst or a project manager.

It shouldn't be necessary for the change manager to intervene on behalf of the change author and obtain this information directly, but they might expect to offer advice on who to ask for further input if necessary. Ultimately, someone has proposed the change for good reason, and they are the primary source. Shortcomings should be treated as learning and improvement opportunities. Training should address this too. It is not the change manager's job to fill in the gaps.

Gathering the risks and considering their mitigation should begin at the start of the process – before a change is even proposed for approval – and should certainly not be left for verbal discussion at the change advisory board. If risks are not examined early in the process, a change could waste a lot of time and money in development only to be thrown out later because they are too high.

Ideally, risk assessment is best conducted as a joint exercise between IT and the business, to specifically think through the risks and how to mitigate them when considering a change. Leaving risk assessment to be part of a later writing process rarely does it justice, because by then it is one person thinking from their own perspective at that time, although it is important to review and update risks in light of technical developments.

While it is not necessary, or possible, to identify every single risk, neither is it acceptable to think of a couple and move on, happy that there are some words in the field. Put another way: the requirements of the request for change should inform the development of a change from its initiation, not be reverse-engineered at the last minute to satisfy the process! As with everything, the change manager should be thorough in their acceptance of risk assessments and strive to embed the requirements of the process into the natural workflow of those making changes.

Test plan 1

A large part of the mitigation of risk will be the test plan. Again, the author of the request for change can seek input from others if they are not responsible for everything. This could include dedicated test management, overall project management or a team leader. It really depends on the scale of the operation and how things are done locally.

Testing at this stage refers to the dry run of the change. This might be code testing in software development or building the change in an environment that has no impact on live business operations. This test plan should provide explicit instructions for the tester to follow. What is needed in the request for change is some evidence to support its success as a way of mitigating the risks involved in live implementation. A request for change shouldn't be approved for implementation until the successful outcome of testing is known.

The test plan to confirm successful change should be described explicitly in the request for change – see Test plan 2 below.

Implementation plan

The implementation plan in a request for change should provide all the information that the implementer will need on the day.

This includes the steps for the tasks to be performed, in order of performance; timings; sources or locations of items required; plus any additional instructions from external sources. It may be easier to produce the implementation plan outside the request for change as a separate pack of documentation, but the request for change must refer to it and it must be available to reviewers and approvers.

If the information provided is incomplete or unconvincing, the change manager must return it for update, providing guidance on what is needed if necessary. If an inadequate implementation plan gets past the change manager, reviewers and approvers are empowered to reject it. Indeed, it is why they are there, but that is not to say that the change manager should not aim to prevent this by adding value in quality checks. That is why the change manager is there, to ease the process.

Test plan 2
This is the testing that is carried out to confirm successful implementation of the change after the implementation plan has been followed. The test plan should be specific enough for the tester or implementer to follow explicitly, because approval is granted based on what will happen on the day. It may be appropriate to refer out to a master test plan, but all reviewers and approvers, as well as the change manager, must be able to consider it in conjunction with the request for change.

Contingency plan
The contingency plan is commonly referred to as the 'back-out plan' or 'fall-back plan'. It is the remediation plan for what the implementer will do if the change goes wrong on the day and must return services to their pre-change state, consider a deviation from the implementation plan to complete the change or park it in an acceptable state.

Special attention should be given to the availability of the components that will be needed if the contingency plan is invoked. Will the implementer be able to access everything they need immediately? Is it necessary to locate items in advance of the change as preparation, just in case? It may be too late to leave it to chance on the day and this risks services being unavailable for longer than estimated, possibly cutting into agreed service time.

The contingency plan should contain explicit instructions on how to reverse the implementation and include guidance for escalating the possibility of deviation from the implementation plan, to mitigate the circumstances. For example, it may be necessary to involve more senior technical input as well as managers to agree a way forward, or business representatives to grant or deny further downtime, or both. The change manager should be involved in such decisions.

Effectively, deviation from the plan becomes an emergency change in its variation, or it is backed out as failed or partially failed without deviation taking place. The scale and risk of the change should determine the extent of the drama required in the event of full or partial change failure. In some cases, the implementer may be empowered to make the judgements necessary. More information on scale and risk is provided in the next section.

The change manager should ensure that the contingency plan is comprehensive so that any need to reverse the change is as risk free as possible. 'Contingency' is a good word to use when advising change requesters if they are struggling to understand the concept or the need. The terms 'back-out', 'fall-back' and 'remediation' all hint at inevitability, whereas 'contingency' suggests what it is – **in case** something goes wrong, not **when** something goes wrong. It is a safety net, not a foregone conclusion.

A comprehensive contingency plan can be used to mitigate risks identified in the risk assessment and adds further value to the change planning process in this respect.

Scale and risk
Changes are sometimes classified as major or minor as a way of identifying scale at a glance and as a way of differentiating between workflows. For example, a minor change may require fewer approval stages or less-senior involvement.

This classification might be automatically applied through the configuration of a change management system depending on criteria selected, or it might be manually entered or selected by the requester according to the tools in use and the procedure defined.

Sometimes it might depend on a matrix calculation based on the impact of a change and the degree of risk, which could result in more profiles to label and assign. This is a local process interpretation. Figure 4.3 shows a simple example.

Figure 4.3 A typical risk and impact matrix

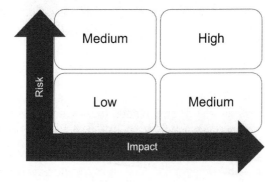

In the example, a change that is low risk and low impact has an overall rating of Low; low risk and medium impact or medium risk and low impact is rated Medium, and medium risk and medium impact is High. These might be translated into minor, moderate and major changes.

In any case, the change manager should validate the selections and final categorisation. It can be tempting (for some) to try and shortcut the process by being less than thorough in interpretation of the impact and risks!

Priority
Priority is another subjective classification. Everyone's change is urgent to them, so appropriate selection can be problematic. It can be helpful for the change manager to

publish some criteria to support this. This is especially true where emergencies are concerned. Ultimately, priority relates to overall business impact and provides a way to order the changes for review, approval and scheduling.

Fast-track changes are subject to explicit classification, as such, and delegate authority to requesters to prioritise these changes themselves, provided they meet the pre-approved criteria. For example, they must be implemented in acknowledged maintenance windows. The systematic assessment of frequently occurring changes and their promotion to fast-track status keeps the process lean and primed to focus on those that are more complex. Without this, there is a risk that changes will become bogged down in a pipeline that is bloated with repetition.

Review, approval and implementation details

Peer review
Peer review is a useful step, especially when preparing new or complex changes. This requires someone with comparable technical ability to review the plans for change and suggest improvements or highlight risks. This can be a useful way to share knowledge and double-check risk assessments. It is not intended as a slight on the capability of the author, but as a second pair of eyes looking to see what might have been missed. It can be a good way of mitigating the risk of the change manager becoming a single point of failure – if everything is reviewed only by the change manager, there is a chance that something will slip through the net. Fast-track changes should no longer need peer review.

Approvals
The levels of approval required for requests for change will be determined locally. It is reasonable to expect a wide range of representation for technical, management, financial, business and customers.

There should be at least two stages of approval: one to authorise preparing the change and one to authorise implementation. Each stage may have multiple approvers.

The selection of approvers will most likely depend on the scale and risk profile of each change. Major changes could require more senior approval than minor changes or may need a wider consensus. Minor changes might be nodded through by local managers or team leaders.

Major changes, at least, might be expected to be presented at a change advisory board meeting, for discussion if necessary, although attendees should be prepared with their opinions, questions and decisions. If a change has been approved between meetings without further question, it should typically be ratified at the CAB so that there is a record of its approval in the meeting minutes. Sometimes it is necessary to discuss and agree the scheduling of the change. Often, minor changes can be pushed through between meetings but they should make an appearance in terms of status regardless of that.

The change manager always confirms approval before implementation can take place, even if other approvers have done their bit – the change manager is the ultimate approver. Recording approvals is best supported by a dedicated change management workflow system but the process can be made to work using basic tools such as documents, emails and spreadsheets. It is good practice to put in place some form of document management to show traceability of decisions. This can be useful if there are problems resulting from change after the event, as well as being a vital record of evidence for auditors.

Sometimes a change advisory board meeting might approve a change 'subject to' something being done. This can be a helpful way of keeping changes flowing, rather than being held up or postponed until the next meeting. The change manager is expected to ratify that whatever was promised to secure approval is carried out, and recorded on the request for change, before they give the nod to proceed. This approach comes into its own when there are a lot of approvers or CAB members who can be difficult to pin down between meetings. It gives the change manager a realistic way of keeping to schedules without having to metaphorically or literally walk an updated RFC around every approver office after a meeting has disbanded, which is not a good use of their time, or the approvers' time, and effectively turns the changes into emergencies.

Efficiency and pragmatism keep the process flowing and help to prevent bottlenecks, provided that looser controls are not abused.

The change advisory board and what it involves is discussed later in this chapter.

Implementation outcome

The author or implementer of the change should update the request for change with the outcome of implementation. They should provide details of actuality against plan, recording details of any deviation that became necessary to complete a change successfully.

Any deviation that takes place should do so in accordance with the contingency plan approved thus far in the request for change. Since it is difficult to legislate for all eventualities, and the implementation plan is expected to succeed, it may be that the contingency plan is escalated through functional and hierarchical routes to agree next steps at the point of failure. The change manager should be involved to make sure that the correct process is followed for further change.

Usually a request for change will be classified as complete, with variations such as 'fully successful', 'partially successful' or 'failed', for the purpose of reporting. Confirmation of completion of any associated tasks should also be recorded; for example, updating documents and databases.

The change manager should be able to expect outcome updates on a request for change soon after the event, if not immediately, as this provides the formal communication on the outcome and should trigger timely updates to configuration records.

Post-implementation review

Post-implementation review may form part of the implementation update, if it is a straightforward report that can be provided by the same person. In most cases it should be cursory, with nothing adverse to report following a wholly successful change.

If a formal post-implementation review meeting is being convened by the change manager, because it requires wide and varied contributions, it is likely that the change manager will summarise the findings of the review in the request for change.

Post-implementation review should address any lessons learned as a result of the change. This applies even if the change was successful, in the end, since any deviation from plan should provide input to future planning. Post-implementation review is discussed in more detail later in this chapter.

Completion and closure

Completion flags a request for change as ready for closure. This interim step can be used to retain visibility of a change at the change advisory board meeting until closure is acknowledged. This ensures that attendees are explicitly aware of the end of a change, rather than it just dropping off the agenda.

Closure is the final act on a request for change and it reflects a status change for reporting purposes. It can be used to filter out changes no longer requiring discussion or approval. The date of closure is normally included for reporting purposes as well.

The change manager should be responsible for closing requests for change, having first checked that all other expectations have been met.

CHANGE ADVISORY BOARD

The change advisory board, or CAB, is a meeting held regularly by the change manager to discuss changes at various stages of proposal, planning, approval and completion. The selection of participants in the CAB will be a point of local discussion and agreement, but it is likely to include a range of change approvers representing technical teams, customer-facing teams, management, financial authority and the business. Attendance is not limited to approvers; there may be participants who wish to attend for information only, and change authors or representatives may attend to answer questions or hear the result.

How often the CAB meeting takes place will also be a local decision and will depend on the typical throughput of change. Little and often keeps things moving and weekly is not unusual. Matching development life cycles is a good idea; remember the change process should deliver change, not obstruct it, so having a frequent enough CAB meeting to support Agile methods may be helpful. If longer timescales are involved, it might be better to hold them less frequently when the time spent on them will be more productive than if nothing much has moved on since the last meeting. Of course, it is necessary to consider all requirements, not just those of development teams, so the change manager should consider all of these before imposing any plan.

It is advisable to stick to a regular frequency unless throughput is such that only ad hoc meetings are required. Chopping and changing makes it difficult for attendees to plan and reliability encourages attendance. The best approach is to block-book a range of dates and arrange any meeting rooms required at the same time. Then publish a schedule, so everyone knows what they are committed to and where they have to be.

It is common for invited attendees to have one or more deputies to cover for them in their absence because it is important that each approver area is always represented. However, the change manager should be mindful of regular dilution of authority. Those who do attend must be empowered to make decisions about changes. If deputies must report back for a decision, this is defeating the purpose of the meeting and waiting for follow-up can delay the process unacceptably.

Service desk representation

Always make sure that the service desk is represented and empowered to contribute to decisions at the change advisory board meeting. The service desk will be the first point of contact if there is a problem following a change, and they may also take calls from end-users needing help with new services. The service desk must feel suitably prepared to deal with these and should have an opportunity to confirm this before an implementation goes ahead.

Business change and digital transformation programmes or projects should have factored in these aspects as part of the overall planning, but representation at CAB level ensures that they have a say on readiness, even if they are not on the approval workflow for individual changes.

Administration

In addition to arranging meetings and identifying participants, the change manager is responsible for the agenda and minutes of the CAB.

The agenda should provide enough information for participants to be able to identify the changes that are relevant to them, review them adequately before each meeting and form an opinion to express on the day.

The physical agenda might be a report that can be defined in the change management system or through the use of reporting tools. It will usually be presented as columns of data, including type of change, priority, title and summary, proposed schedule and status. Items might be sorted by group – for example, major and minor changes – or by priority; whatever best helps to organise the meeting. You might want to release senior approvers after the major changes have been discussed, for instance, and putting all the major changes at the top of the agenda sets the format to enable them to leave early.

If dedicated change management tools are not used, a spreadsheet can provide similar functionality.

A record should be made of decisions and actions to be taken after the meeting. Even if participants make their own notes, the change manager must have an overall view of what happens next, because they must be able to validate it. They will also have actions themselves – to move changes to approved status where they are the next point in the chain, for example.

The meeting record can follow a similar format to the agenda. If updates can be entered directly on to requests for change in a change management system during the meeting, it should be possible to generate general reports that pull out the key information as a summary report afterwards. Otherwise it will be necessary to take notes during the meeting for compilation later.

Rolling agenda and minutes

It can be useful to use the meeting record from one meeting as the basis of the agenda for the next meeting. This is especially helpful if the same changes are reviewed from one week to the next, because it should provide a summary of the previous discussion and decisions, to avoid going over old ground.

The danger with this is that the agenda can become very long if changes are carried forward repeatedly. However, it does highlight the tendency and can be a trigger to consider the cause of this and improve the process. Perhaps the CAB is not frequent enough for the throughput of work, or meeting attendees are unprepared to approve changes and defer them to the next meeting, or there is insufficient information on requests for change to warrant approval, or something else. You investigate and decide!

Facilitation

The change manager is also expected to run the CAB meeting. They will start the meeting, work through the agenda, engage participants and summarise conclusions, checking agreement as the meeting progresses. They will close the meeting and remind participants of the date of the next meeting.

Setting expectations

Appropriate participation is crucial to the smooth running of the CAB and the change management process. Attendees should have read the agenda and the requests for change listed in advance and be ready to contribute their decisions. They should not attend blind and expect to be spoon-fed the details at the meeting. Although it is reasonable to invite change authors to clarify for the benefit of all in some situations, it should not become necessary to explain the detail of every change for real-time consideration. If this happens the meetings will soon become lengthy and cumbersome, and if they start to take up too much time people will be discouraged from attending, especially those who do take the time to prepare adequately.

The change manager leads the CAB and should set expectations from the outset. Don't assume that everyone knows what is expected of them; make it clear (politely) at the first meeting so there can be no misunderstanding.

It can also be frustrating to try and run a meeting where attendees divide their attention between the meeting and their laptop or other device. How you can handle this will depend on the prevailing culture, but asking for full attention should be reasonable and in everyone's interests for getting the most from the meetings and the time available. Demonstrating good management of meetings is a transferrable skill to be cultivated in any case. Be assertive and polite and your position should be respected by all attendees, regardless of their seniority.

Expecting management commitment to efficient meetings is reasonable, and management commitment in general is an important aspect of a successful change management process. This is looked at as a specific topic later in this chapter.

Keeping meetings to time can be difficult if there are a lot of participants and, as the subject matter is variable, each meeting discussion will be different. It only takes one contentious change to bring out multiple queries and objections that derail the timetable and make the meeting overrun. The change manager should run a tight ship in respect of meeting management. Repeated overruns will frustrate participants, who may feel that they must stay whatever the impact on their next activity or they may feel they must leave before the end, which will disrupt the CAB and its ability to manage the change process.

Change manager preparation will help in these situations. It should be possible to get a feel for the temperature in advance of the meeting and take pre-emptive action if possible. For example, major changes on high-profile systems, big projects or emergency changes can be red flags and it may help to gauge any issues in advance of the CAB and invite a speaker to field them. The change manager should also be familiar enough with the agenda to know where the peaks and troughs are and manage time accordingly. Grouping some minor changes at the start and marching the meeting through them quickly so there is time to devote to the hot potato can stop the little ones falling out of the end of the meeting. This should keep everyone happy.

Multitasking

Running the change advisory board meeting requires 100% attention from the change manager. If the change manager is also the scribe, this can make for slow progress as everyone must pause while the change manager writes down, or types, the outcome and actions. This can be mitigated if you are using dedicated change management software tools and can update records in real time during the meeting but, even then, there is a danger that there will be long periods of silence while you write down the thinking!

Ideally someone other than the change manager should take the notes or update the system, even if the change manager writes them up afterwards. If there is no one else directly on the change management team, and no administrators are available to support you, ask participants to take it in turns. You will need to carefully summarise outcomes for the record to make sure that everyone has the same understanding, but this can be a good thing – to avoid misunderstandings in general.

Alternatively, you could make an audio recording that you can play back and transcribe, although this can be time-consuming. Audio recordings alone don't provide the summary information needed by participants and the wider audience. Using a combination of audio recording and a willing meeting participant could be a good compromise so that you can refer to the audio if the written notes are unclear or incomplete.

There is a lot to be said for preparing the agenda yourself as a way of immersing yourself in the content. It makes for a smooth meeting if you know what's coming. If you delegate agenda preparation as well as the minutes, you should rehearse your presentation to avoid hesitation. Participants need to feel confident that the change manager is familiar with plans.

CHANGE SCHEDULE

Although the minutes of the CAB meetings are normally circulated to meeting attendees, and circulation could be widened for information if necessary, it is good practice to produce a separate change schedule as a much shorter summary of the changes that are ready to go and which have a time slot.

This is useful for those at the sharp end of implementation, who just want the headlines. They will refer to their detailed requests for change for the specifics of the job. They don't want to wade through the whys and wherefores of the decision-making process, they just want to know the decision and when they get to roll up their sleeves.

It is also useful to make a version of the change schedule available to the business – as a similar summary – focusing on information of specific interest to them such as what is new following the change, when and for how long any service outages will be, and contact details for more information.

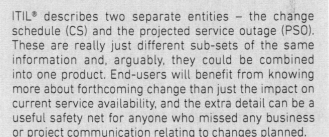

Change schedule and projected service outage

ITIL® describes two separate entities – the change schedule (CS) and the projected service outage (PSO). These are really just different sub-sets of the same information and, arguably, they could be combined into one product. End-users will benefit from knowing more about forthcoming change than just the impact on current service availability, and the extra detail can be a useful safety net for anyone who missed any business or project communication relating to changes planned.

For more information on ITIL® change management see ITIL® Service Transition.[2]

---

2 www.tsoshop.co.uk/AXELOS-Global-Best-Practice/ITIL/#Service-Transition

For minimum effort, the change schedule (and projected service outage) can become a rolling document that is kept up to date in real time and stored where everyone can see it and knows where to find it. Every time a change is approved (bearing in mind that this might be a fast-track or minor change that is approved between CAB meetings), the change schedule is updated. It is probably a good idea to limit the schedule to only positive notices; if you want to include everything that is in the pipeline, with tentative implementation dates or not, approvals or not, you might as well issue the CAB agenda and minutes to all. There is no reason why you can't do this if you wish.

Depending on the tools used to share this information, it might be necessary to schedule a regular notification of some kind (email will do), to make sure it gets seen on a regular basis. It is not reasonable to expect everyone in the business to check in on it all the time, just in case something has appeared. If weekends are popular times for changes, Friday morning might be a good slot for this.

You might send a notification to change implementers as an update after the CAB meeting as well. Of course, if your weekend change schedule is evolving right up to Friday close-of-business, you might need to be more dynamic in how the latest plan is communicated.

Don't forget the service desk!

POST-IMPLEMENTATION REVIEW

A post-implementation review is carried out after every change and the findings are recorded on the request for change document. At its simplest, a post-implementation review is a statement of fact that a change has been implemented successfully and this is normally done by the person implementing the change or change author, not the change manager. It is a standard part of every change process and a precursor to completion and closure.

However, if a change fails, either fully or partially, or the change succeeds with ad hoc approval for deviation from the implementation or contingency plans the change manager should at least be in the loop of the post-implementation review, to make sure that lessons learned are identified and shared for the benefit of all.

For a relatively minor change where there was no impact on services – for example, one in which the change was backed-out successfully – review and re-planning would probably be left to the change team involved. The change manager would be made aware and the request for change would be updated as a failed or partially failed change, with post-implementation review findings added, before it was closed. This would be acknowledged at the following CAB meeting, which would ensure its dissemination. Normally, a new request for change would be raised for the next attempt, with reference to the original, and the lessons learned would be reflected in the new impact and risk assessments, plans for testing, implementation and back-out, and so on.

For major changes that fail or cause an impact on services, the change manager is more closely involved in order to understand what went wrong, co-ordinate lessons learned and communicate with the wider business on behalf of the process and its participants. Depending on the scale and severity of the fallout, the change manager might convene a post-implementation review meeting to bring all parties with evidence together to map out the full picture of events, before drawing conclusions and sharing lessons learned. In such cases, the change manager should take responsibility for recording the findings of the discussion and updating the request for change. They should also retain a record of the meeting and share relevant information with those affected by disruption to services. This should include any IT representatives, such as business relationship managers, service level managers and the service desk, as well as business stakeholders.

Major incidents

Major incidents can occur all on their own. They are not always caused by a change. Managing major incidents usually involves a formal process to work through the issue, put in a temporary or permanent solution, restore service and, usually, hold a review of what happened, to understand the impact, identify lessons for the future and provide explanations to the business.

Major incidents are usually managed by an individual representing the reactive process of getting things back up and running; they will coordinate the diagnosis and resolution, and schedule and deliver regular progress reports to all stakeholders. Their role is to protect those at the sharp end, who are trying to implement a fix as quickly as possible, from all-comers looking for the latest information. It might be fulfilled by someone such as a service desk manager or problem manager.

Major incidents are similar to the post-implementation reviews held by a change manager following fallout from a failed change. The change manager can expect to be included in major incident reviews, because resolution of a major incident will almost certainly involve the emergency change process. In this respect, the change manager will front the emergency request(s) for change and will be a key player in the major incident review because they will have been directly involved in the diagnosis of the cause and the solution implemented.

In this case it makes sense to combine the post-implementation review of the emergency change(s) with the major incident review as a whole, with the major incident manager taking the lead. However, the change manager is a good choice for an alternative major incident manager if one needs to be identified, because of the obvious synergies between the two processes.

PROCESS IMPLEMENTATION

This section contains some general tips on implementing and improving a change management process that encourages cooperation. Even if you inherit a process, it is never 'finished' and you can apply the principles at any stage because they are about approaches rather than the process itself.

Good practice

Don't reinvent the wheel. For details on typical process steps for change management, ITIL® Service Transition[3] is a good source. ITIL® Practitioner Guidance[4] also provides a comprehensive set of principles for applying its processes to local needs.

Consultation

Always consult stakeholder representatives first. If you are considering change management policy, designing a process, thinking about improvements to what is already there, or planning anything that you are expecting others to participate in, always consult with them before you start. Even if your plans reflect your area of expertise and you are empowered to do as you wish, consulting stakeholders will ensure that (a) you don't overlook anything that they need that you weren't aware of and (b) they will be more likely to participate willingly when your plans are implemented.

Even if you suspect that no one has a clue what they want, go through the motions anyway because the first time you don't will be the time someone says: 'you didn't ask me'. Even if you present a first draft for comment, anything you have missed looks like

---

3   www.tsoshop.co.uk/AXELOS-Global-Best-Practice/ITIL/#Service-Transition

4   www.tsoshop.co.uk/AXELOS-Global-Best-Practice/ITIL/#ITIL-Practitioner-Guidance

exclusion from the start, however accidental it was. There is no need to spend a lot of time on it, just make it the first thing you do. A short email with a meaningful subject line (so it doesn't get ignored), setting out your objective and asking for specific needs, with a reasonable deadline for response, is enough to show you care. Don't try and slip it past with an unremarkable subject line in the interests of expediency. Don't be tempted to let cynicism creep in by asking questions and answering them in the same breath. Ask the questions and wait for the deadline to pass.

But don't expect too much. Not everyone has time for a blank sheet of paper (but everyone does like to be asked). You can send out a reminder closer to your deadline, letting them know that you will circulate a draft based on your understanding of requirements, with or without responses. Have one you prepared earlier if you like, ready to send out, but remember to update it to reflect any contributions you do get. Ask for comment and give a reasonable deadline for response. Make it easy for people to discuss it with you. Give them every opportunity to contribute. Only when you have exhausted consultation options openly should you move on to setting out your own interpretation.

It can be tempting to cut out this step as a waste of time, especially if you are under time pressure yourself, but it is a crucial step to getting buy-in to your finished policy/process/ new request for change template/meeting format. It is better, and often quicker in the long term, to factor in the extra time at the start than to have to start again at the end. Don't feel you have to wait forever or labour the point if there is no response but be open and transparent from the start and publicise widely.

Be sincere

If you don't ask people what they think right at the start, they will look and feel like an afterthought if you ask them later, even if you always intended to ask them. Acting first suggests that you are not really interested in what they think because you made a start without them. It's not about what you meant, but how it looks.

Management commitment

Make sure you know what it looks like and make sure you have it.

Management commitment means that managers walk-the-walk as well as talk-the-talk on change management. Lip-service in public and then pulling rank to bend the rules when it suits is not management commitment. Management commitment means being treated like everyone else, or everyone else will try to bend the rules as well.

You need management commitment from every manager whose teams will take part, and from your own manager(s) so that they stand up for the process when those not committed to it try to go around you. Management commitment forms part of the defence. Weak links are doors to kick open; if they are firmly shut, those looking for them will learn not to expect special treatment.

The best way to ensure management commitment is to involve all managers in the design and implementation from the start.

Ways of saying no

Culture doesn't change overnight, and old ways of working can be hard to shake off. New regimes can seem like a slight. Sometimes, the benefit of the doubt isn't earned. It can be frustrating to be faced with repeated requests to make an exception to the process and tempting to just refuse. Unfortunately, that can often make things worse and send the protagonist up the management hierarchy.

You have nothing to fear if your manager is committed, but you risk the wrath of everyone whose time is wasted to reach the same conclusion. Do what you can to persuade and cajole. If necessary, try to compromise without undermining the process. If a change is a legitimate emergency, then help to put the request through the emergency process to demonstrate that it works.

Adopt your own best practice

A good approach to implementing a change management process that does not represent too much change for people is to start where they are. Canvas the technical teams in all areas and ask how they plan, build and implement changes already. Pay special attention to the timescales of life cycles; this is especially important if Agile methodologies are in full swing already. Pool your findings and use them to create a local 'best practice' process, made up of the best bits from everywhere, and, in the interests of fairness, try and include something from everyone if you can.

You can still use a good practice framework, such as ITIL®, as a checklist to plug any gaps but by starting with current practice, and listening to hard won expertise that is already available in the context of the organisation, you are not perceived as throwing out perfectly good ways of doing things for the sake of fashion, or suggesting that you know best and they know nothing. Taking this approach will mean that people will still have to change some of the things they do, but less is more.

Remember that it doesn't have to be perfect from the start (if ever) and something that is used consistently by everyone is better than everyone doing their own thing, so don't exclude something that can be improved as time goes by, especially if it helps someone feel they have contributed.

Making it work for everyone

Change management is just another cog in the business machine. It is no use to anyone if it is a lone cog spinning happily on its own; it must engage with the other cogs in the machine to add any value to what they are doing. Without them it has no purpose; they are the reason for its existence.

That's a good perspective to keep in mind. The change manager cog needs the other cogs to justify its own existence and, given what has been said about change management often being an afterthought, the machine has probably already found a way to work without it (it just breaks down more often).

If change management is to add value, the change manager must help the business machine find a way to incorporate it. The change manager should not roll out an arbitrary process and expect everyone else to adapt to fit it. Practically, this means going to the teams developing changes and grafting the connections between them, not just trying to bolt it on the end. Invite yourself to their meetings. Find ways to blend in. Avoid making them come to you. Find and make opportunities to suggest ways of working together.

Project management methodologies already perform risk management in their own life cycles, so work with them to embed the change management requirements into their own practice. They shouldn't have to repeat themselves; once is enough. Find a way to apply what they do naturally to the change management life cycle, not the other way around. Testing? Already a mature concept in software development; help them to align the needs of change management to the development process so that it is an automatic by-product, not a new hoop to jump through.

In the end, the more the change manager can bind the change management process into existing ways of working, the more successful the process will be. The benefits will be seen, but protests of extra work and bureaucracy will be less likely to be heard.

Factor in change management

Make sure that the requirements of the request for change are considered from the start of change planning, and developed alongside it, not written as an afterthought to comply with a separate process.

Accessibility

Making it work for everyone means more than just integrating current practice. You must also make the process suitable for a diversity of needs. For example, the ability to interact with tools requires consideration if everyone is to have equal access to the process. The Web Content Accessibility Guidelines (WCAG)[5] are a good place to start for good practice but talk to those whose needs you are trying to meet, who will know more about what works for them than you.

Accessible or inclusive

Making something accessible suggests adapting it for additional or specific needs. Making something inclusive suggests a design that meets all needs without adaptation.

It should be possible to design new systems to be inclusive; remember to consult those with needs at the start. Legacy systems may require adaptation or additional support; remember to consult those with needs at the start!

Training

Competence is something that the change manager must ensure for the success of the process, and if they need to train contributors then they should. However, that does not mean they should not allow them to learn about change management of their own volition too. Top-down organisational culture for learning and development can co-exist with an individual ethic of making knowledge widely available and the change manager should make it as easy as possible for participants to find out what they need to know.

---

5 www.w3.org/WAI/standards-guidelines/wcag/

Competence vs competency

Competence and competency are often used interchangeably; the *Oxford English Dictionary* conflates them.[6] The subtle difference is that competence refers to the requirements of the practitioner, whereas competencies are the behaviours the practitioner demonstrates.

As the change manager, you are responsible for change management training. There may be a learning and development department or a dedicated technical trainer who will translate your needs and act on your behalf in your organisation. Or you might have to do it yourself. But there must be some localised intervention; generic change management training is only good for a generic overview – it won't tell people how your process works with your tools. But training should be as light as possible, with back-up reference material for just-in-time answers to immediate questions. It shouldn't really be necessary to get people into a classroom or subject them to death-by-slideshow. Aim instead to produce a brief overview of the policy and process with a set of pared down, fit-for-purpose instructions for everything they will need to do – from getting an account on the system, if you have one, to closing their first request for change and everything in between.

Think of it as technical documentation. Put yourself in the shoes of the change author and write what they need to know – no more, no less. If the reader is expected to follow your instructions to operate onscreen actions, it should not be necessary to pad the documentation out with shots of every screen. They can see them in real life as they go and shouldn't need a 20-page document when a one-page crib-sheet will do. Screen shots only add value to highlight something that is

---

6   https://en.oxforddictionaries.com/definition/competence

otherwise difficult to locate, which good user interface design should avoid. But remember that this may not be appropriate for all – see the section on **accessibility** above.

If you are using a dedicated change management system, it should be possible to embed guidance and help into the workflow to direct people as they work through the process, which might serve as a suitable alternative to separate instructions. This is for training purposes though; you should still document your process and procedures (see **Chapter 3**). Producing a variety of complementary methods is the best approach, for individual selection according to need and context.

Testing, testing ...

Always have someone unfamiliar with the process test your instructions. It doesn't matter how well you think you have captured them – you already know the process and can't be objective.

For further guidance on writing instructions, the BCS guide *Technical Writing for Business People*[7] is a good source.

KEY POINTS

- The request for change is the primary vehicle in the change management process.

- The more the change management process is embedded into existing ways of working, the more successful it will be.

- Implementing the process is best done collaboratively.

---

7 www.bcs.org/books/technicalwriting

5   TOOLS

Dedicated software tools for change management will make the job as easy as possible, but it is not essential to have them. A small organisation may not be able to justify the expense and may not have the throughput of change to warrant complicated workflows and multiple templates. This chapter looks at what is available for professional deployment and what can be used in the smaller scale or to prove the concept before investing further.

CHANGE MANAGEMENT SOFTWARE TOOLS

Change management is supported by well-established software tools from a range of suppliers, through traditional local deployments or software-as-a-service (SaaS). They are popularly available as modules of integrated IT service management systems that can be purchased as a single process or as clusters of processes. See later in this chapter for further information on integrated systems.

The core functionality for a change management software tool is workflow that allows the configuration of multiple routes for requests for change, starting with the change author and navigating stages through reviews, approvals, evaluation of change and closure, depending on the nature of the change and who the stakeholders are on a case-by-case basis.

Features normally include the ability to configure standard (fast-track) changes, tracking to identify potential collisions between changes, configurable data sets and standard reporting. Some software tools have change advisory board tools for creating a meeting agenda and recording notes, as well as a calendar for scheduling changes. CAB facilities can be especially helpful if you can project the system during the meeting to help you stay on top of updates in real time.

Maximum benefit is derived from change management software when it is integrated with a configuration management system. It then becomes possible to associate requests for change with configuration items, identify risks and impact, and detect unauthorised changes, depending on the solution chosen.

Choosing the right tool

Should you define the process and buy a tool that fits, or buy a tool to guide your process? There is no correct answer to this. It can be tempting to be led by what is on the market, and there is some sense in this, but there are pitfalls too. Configurability is important, as this will determine your reporting capability, and if you don't have some idea of how you will configure the software, how do you know you have chosen the right tool?

However, IT service management tools, including change management, have been around for a long time now and there is nothing wrong with taking a steer from what they can do. If you are new to the field, it makes no sense to waste time dreaming up an ideal solution when so much is already on offer.

It is reasonable to look at the market to get an idea of what is available and how prices might vary accordingly. But it always pays to then define **your** process to inform your requirements before you shortlist and compare offerings. You may find there is nothing between them in terms of functionality and choice will come down to other factors, such as look and feel, ease with which you can (re)configure it, customer support and price.

If you don't define your process before you make your final choice, you run the risk of getting distracted by shiny things and inflating your needs unrealistically. It is then tempting to buy beyond your needs, and means, on the grounds that you will 'grow into it', but instead get bogged down at the specification stage, extend your implementation period and fail to realise the benefits quickly, only to have no time left anyway to deploy the shiny things. By the time you get around to it there may be a new version out, so you might as well have waited.

CONFIGURATION MANAGEMENT SYSTEM

As mentioned earlier in the book, configuration management is a separate process, but it is closely associated with change management. Configuration management is about building a representation of the IT estate in records called configuration items, where a configuration item has a sub-set of attributes.

Example configuration item record

Attributes	Configuration item type: laptop
Unique ID	ABC123456
Make	Wizzo
Model	Super-wiz
Serial number	987-654321
Memory	8GB
SSD	240GB
HDD	1TB

Configuration item records might be linked to other configuration item records to represent how they work together. In the example shown, a laptop configuration item record might be linked to software licences representing the software installed on it and the current owner. Software licences would have a different set of attributes, such as licence number and associated media, including any documents. Owner would be another set, with attributes such as location, department and telephone number.

This is a simplified example, but you can see how you can build up a representation of the organisation through its IT equipment, which extends to the wider infrastructure and services. This is the configuration management system, sometimes known as the configuration management database, and it can be used as the basis for planning changes; in order to be effective, it must be updated when changes are implemented. The change management process, therefore, is essential in keeping the CMS up to date.

Be careful what you wish for

It is easy to get carried away designing and developing a CMS but the more you include, the more you must keep up to date. If the CMS is not kept fully up to date, or is only even slightly mistrusted, it is not possible to plan changes confidently on any of it.

The best way to keep the CMS up to date is through change management, which means that everything that is recorded in the CMS – every CI and every attribute – must require a request for change before it can proceed. Many of these can probably be designed as fast-track requests for change but there is still an effort overhead on those responsible, without full automation.

Remember this when designing a CMS and only record that which is genuinely useful to know and track, or risk bringing the organisation to a standstill – literally. At least start small and build in a controlled way.

Closing the loop on changes and updating the status of configuration items in a timely manner means that next time a change is proposed it is planned on accurate information, and information about any issues that occurred should be visible in the previous post-implementation review. In this way, impact and risk assessments get better and traction on continual improvement becomes automatic.

CMS records can also be used to identify unauthorised changes. If the record doesn't match the reality when a change is implemented, this suggests that the physical item has been changed without an update to the CMS, which should in turn suggest that the change management process has been bypassed. Or it might mean that the record update part of the process has failed. Either way there is a clue to follow.

Rights

To be confident of the integrity of the CMS, it is important to restrict access rights so that it is not widely open to unauthorised updates. Updates should only happen as a result of completed requests for change. If the CMS can be updated in any other way, you lose your ability to monitor unauthorised change.

The CMS provides a central repository of information about configuration items. The information stored here is useful for those planning changes, as well as for other processes implemented in integrated systems. CMS software usually comes with change management and integrated IT service management software tools.

INTEGRATED IT SERVICE MANAGEMENT SOFTWARE TOOLS

Integrated IT service management tools incorporate change management and configuration management into a wider set of processes. Typically, these include incident management, problem management, service catalogues and service level management, and they might extend to other service management processes, such as release management and knowledge management.

Often, it is possible to buy into integrated systems by starting small with just a few process modules and building the capability over time. Integrated systems are comprehensive service management systems that revolve around a central configuration management system and provide a comprehensive suite of monitoring and reporting tools.

There are many integrated IT service management tools available on the market that are well established. Examples include BMC Remedy, ServiceNow, Cherwell Software, Freshservice, Hornbill, Ivanti and TOPDesk, to name just a few.

ITSM tool comparison

As you might expect, there is much to be found in an internet search to help you find and choose a product. Gartner is a long-established and reliable source of guidance and their vendor reviews can be a good place to start.[1]

Another useful source of opinion is the ITSM.tools[2] website, which includes blogs from industry stalwarts as well as reviews of ITSM tools.

The main benefit of integrated systems from the perspective of change management is that change records are available for interrogation by other processes, making it easier to diagnose

---

1   www.gartner.com/reviews/market/it-service-management-tools/vendors

2   See https://itsm.tools/

incidents and problems. Information about incidents and problems are also associated with configuration item records, so those planning changes can see the full picture.

The need for change might be identified through problem diagnosis, and integrated systems provide for inputs from and outputs to other processes, joining them together end to end. For example, an incident might generate a problem investigation that identifies a fault, which in turn generates a change to implement the solution. Integrated systems allow each process to make use of one set of data and provide an overview of all steps.

Where an integrated system is implemented, it is likely that its configuration will be managed centrally and developed according to the needs of all process owners, to enable a consistent but comprehensive solution.

There are open source integrated systems, as well as those that are commercially available. Spiceworks is one such product. However, remember that free to use does not necessarily mean free to support – beware the hidden costs. If you decide on an open source system, choose one that has an active online community for peer support if you prefer not to pay for a support contract (assuming that one is available).

DISCOVERY TOOLS

Discovery tools can be used to gather data about devices connected to a network. This can be a useful way of kick-starting the development of a configuration management system to support the change management process.

Depending on the sophistication of the selected product, discovery tools can provide configuration information as well as device information, including maps of how devices are linked together and information about what is installed on them.

This is also useful for detecting unauthorised change when a snapshot of the current state of the network is compared with an earlier version. See process compliance in **Chapter 3**.

Discovery tools often come bundled with network management tools (SolarWinds is a good example), or integrated IT service management systems (such as Ivanti), so they might already be available in the organisation. There are also open source and low-cost versions available, some with free trials or limited deployment. Examples include Spiceworks and Zenmap.

REPORTING TOOLS

Most change management and integrated IT service management software tools come with at least some predefined reports to use out of the box. Alternatively, you can define and create your own with third-party products.

Don't confuse reporting with dashboards. Both are useful, but a dashboard will only tell you what is happening in real time, usually as a configurable onscreen layout of modules. A dashboard won't give you historical data or trends – you need reporting for these. Use the dashboard for real-time monitoring.

Unfortunately, many so-called out-of-the box reports in fact require developer skills and this can be a problem if you can't easily access someone, especially if, when you do, they have other priorities. Having a report developer just for change management, or IT service management, might be the case in large organisations, but is often a luxury too far.

Third-party tools are generally available for a wide range of skills. Examples include SAP Business Objects, SAP Crystal Reports, Zoho, and BIRT, which is also open source. Finding the right reporting tool can be even more important than choosing the right process tool if you want to be master of your own destiny. Self-sufficiency means you can play with the options until you are satisfied with the outputs without constantly redefining your requirements for someone else to implement.

If you are not using dedicated software tools, spreadsheets can be a useful way of producing data and graphs. Although this can be time-consuming, it is important to attempt some reporting of the process to identify areas for improvement. If nothing else, this could help you make the case for proper tools.

Keep reporting in perspective

Reporting generally can be very time-consuming, and it is easy to find yourself producing reports that have no value other than looking impressive. Reports are only valid if they are used to identify problems and make improvements, so don't fall into the trap of producing vast amounts of information that no one looks at beyond the pretty graph. Start small and build from there. **Chapter 3** provides some approaches to reporting.

COMMUNICATION TOOLS

Some change management and integrated tools include communication aids such as notification – for example, when a request for change is assigned to someone for action – or for more general dynamic chat.

Many generic communication tools can be deployed effectively to support the change manager to be timely and visible. Ubiquitous email is the obvious and default position. How successfully email communicates with stakeholders in change management will depend on the email culture and the email management capabilities of individuals. An email is only as timely as its reader.

Change management is constant communication in order to crank the handle of change management and keep things moving. The change manager should deploy as many modes of communication as possible to suit the preferences in the organisation, so that communication takes place in a timely and effective way. There are many collaborative software tools available to ease cooperation: Google Docs, Trello and Skype, to name but a few. Enterprise social media tools (for example, Slack) and SMS (short message service) can be useful for putting out change management information to teams or whole organisations.

Other corporate tools, such as intranets and bulletin boards, should be embraced to increase the visibility of change management. No process that is kept a secret is going to be effective. Don't give anyone the opportunity to say: 'no one told me'; transparency is your friend. Demand an intranet page to share process knowledge, contact details, change schedules. Make sure HR include reference to it in their induction pack for joiners. If internal blogging is permitted, share your thoughts, ideas and questions; actively encourage contributions. Write wikis to help people learn how change management works. Make sure your share of the knowledge base is populated and alive with activity. Maintain a high profile with whatever tools are at your disposal.

Above all, set a good example. It should go without saying that face-to-face or telephone conversations are often more productive than sending email and text messages if something needs to be discussed and agreed upon to progress it; if they are used just to avoid confrontation, they will be a false economy. The change manager should lead by example.

MAKING DO (OR PROVING THE CONCEPT BEFORE THE EXPENSE!)

It is always nice to have the proper tools for a job, but change management software tools can be expensive. Also, if you are thinking about change management, it is likely that you also have your eye on other IT service management processes, so it is already costing more.

In a small organisation, or one with a low throughput of change, it may not be possible to justify the cost of dedicated tools, and, in any case, it can help you refine your process and define your requirements if you try it out using readily available tools to begin with.

The request for change is essentially a document template. You can use regular word processing software such as Microsoft Word to create a template and make each request for change available to all stakeholders using cloud-based collaboration tools such as Office 365 or Google Apps, or circulate them by email if you prefer.

You will need to create a central register of requests for change, which can be done using a spreadsheet. Create a column for the key fields that appear on the request for change template and log each request for change as a new row. A unique ID for each will be essential. Include anything you would like to report on – you can sort the data to help you create some basic reports. Figure 5.1 illustrates this idea.

You can use the spreadsheet as the basis for a rolling agenda and minutes for the change advisory board meeting by hiding, filtering and sorting to produce a sub-set of what is up for review. If you are updating the same spreadsheet with the outcomes of the meeting, you are avoiding the extra work of maintaining two separate views.

If you have access to a projector, display monitor or interactive whiteboard, you can put up the spreadsheet for all to see. You should still make available the agenda and requests for change in advance of the meeting, to give everyone an opportunity to review them and consider their responses and any questions they may have. If you run the meeting in this way, it is (just about) feasible to update the record with the outcomes in real time to save you having to do any rewriting after the meeting.

Even if you have every intention of buying a change management or integrated IT service management system, it can be helpful to start in this way if change management is new to your organisation (unless the system you choose is very easy to reconfigure). It is common to want to make changes to templates and workflows after a bit of trial and

Figure 5.1 A basic register of requests for change can be created in a spreadsheet

Register - requests for change

RFC ID	Date created	Type	Cat.	P	Desc.	Imp. date	CAB date	Approval status	Closure date	Owner	RFC status
001	[Date]	Normal	Major	2	[Description]	[Date]	[Date]	[TBA]	[TBA]	[Name]	Open
002	[Date]	Emergency	Major	1	[Description]	[Date]	[Date]	Approved	[Date]	[Name]	Closed
003	[Date]	Fast-track	Minor	3	[Description]	[Date]	[Date]	Approved	[Date]	[Name]	Open

error, and using plain old documents and spreadsheets can sometimes make this easier. Suck it and see for a while before you set things in stone. Don't try and put every change through the process from the beginning. Start small, perhaps with one team, or one type of change, to make it manageable using simple tools.

Another option could be to look at existing tools for possible synergies. Can you make use of an incident management or service desk ticketing system as a trial or permanent solution? If you can create an alternative form, categories and assignment groups, could you use this as a makeshift workflow that is less cumbersome than sharing documents? This can be a good option if everyone is already used to using an existing system. Bending it slightly to manage requests for change can overcome a learning curve and get people up to speed quickly. If the system has some reporting functionality, you might be able to produce a report that generates your CAB agenda as well.

The biggest impact on ease of use when adopting documents and spreadsheets for the change management process is when it comes to including information about configuration items, dependencies and impact of change. Even if a configuration management system exists, it will require a manual look-up and rekeying of data. If the information is scattered through the organisation in various databases, spreadsheets and documents anyway, it will be even more difficult to pull it all together. But it does show the extent of the problem, should you be planning to consolidate your makeshift system into 'proper' tools.

There is a lot to be said for trialling the process using what is available; you can learn so much about what you really need in this way, and it is an opportunity for everyone to contribute their ideas and improvements.

KEY POINTS

- Dedicated change management tools are well established.

- Integrated service management tools can provide seamless transition between other processes and change management, but you should at least include a CMS.

- Trialling the process with simple office productivity tools can be a good way to develop the process before choosing the right tools.

6 STANDARDS AND FRAMEWORKS

Standards and frameworks established over several decades provide plenty of support for change managers in technical change management. This chapter introduces the most relevant. There are many publications and training courses available for detailed guidance.

STANDARDS

ISO is the International Organization for Standardization. It publishes documents that provide requirements, specifications, guidelines or characteristics that can be used consistently to ensure that materials, products, processes and services are fit for their purpose.[1] These documents are available from the ISO online store, or from country-specific member bodies. In the UK, this is the British Standards Institution (BSI).[2] Standards are reviewed regularly to make sure that they remain relevant.

Standards can be used as they are to inform the design of products and services. Independent certification bodies assess and certify conformance to the standard, for a fee. Taking this route requires commitment to internal and certification audits. Certification audits are usually every three years, with annual surveillance audits in between.

---

1   See www.iso.org/home.html

2   See www.bsigroup.com/en-GB/

The main international standards relevant to technical change management are described below. The ISO and BSI websites provide comprehensive information.

ISO/IEC 20000

ISO/IEC 20000 is the international standard for IT service management. It is based around the concept of a service management system (SMS). The standard specifies requirements for the service provider to plan, establish, implement, operate, monitor, review, maintain and improve an SMS. The requirements include the design, transition, delivery and improvement of services to fulfil agreed service requirements.[3]

The requirements and guidance for ISO/IEC 20000 could be used to inform the implementation of good practice change management, but their true benefit lies in the complete system for managing IT services. Technical change management is a sub-set of the full requirement.

ISO 9001

ISO 9001 is the international standard for quality management. Conformance to ISO 9001 demonstrates the ability to consistently provide products and services that meet customer and applicable statutory and regulatory requirements and aims to enhance customer satisfaction through the effective application of the quality management system (QMS), including processes for improvement of the system. The requirements are generic and are intended to apply to any organisation, regardless of its type or size, or the products and services it provides.[4]

ISO 9001 embodies the concept of continual improvement that underpins good practice process management in many disciplines, including IT service management. A change

[3]   See www.iso.org/standard/51986.html

[4]   See www.iso.org/standard/62085.html

manager should demonstrate the continual improvement of the change management process and in an ISO 9001 certified or compliant organisation, they do so as part of the wider quality management system in place.

ISO 44001

ISO 44001 is the international standard for collaborative business relationship management. The standard specifies requirements for the effective identification, development and management of collaborative business relationships within or between organisations.[5]

Although this, too, is not change management specific, its concepts are relevant to the fundamental practice of working together, across an organisation and with partners and suppliers, to achieve a common aim. The adoption of this standard, either formally or informally, indicates a commitment to the type of overall culture that supports a healthy change management approach.

BEST PRACTICE FRAMEWORKS, PROCESSES AND PROCEDURES

Frameworks provide the building-blocks of good practice as defined by the collective wisdom of relevant sections of the industry. In this case, IT service management frameworks include change management as a part of the whole, setting the requirements in the context of other related processes. Frameworks suggest approaches and the adopter is free to pick and choose what they do, but with the advantage of standing on the shoulders of giants. Standards, on the other hand, set out compulsory requirements to establish conformity if certification is desired. It is not possible to be compliant with a framework, which, by definition, is not compulsory. It is not necessary to be compliant with a standard if certification is not

---

5   See www.iso.org/standard/72798.html

required (but it is unethical to claim compliance if the standard is not met).

Processes are the steps taken to turn an input into an output. The incident management process, for example, takes an incident and turns it into a solution. The things that happen between the incident occurring and implementing the solution forms the incident management process. Similarly, the change management process is what happens between identifying a change and reaching its conclusion. Processes are based on the requirements of frameworks, but are not prescribed in frameworks, to allow for individual flexibility. Every organisation is different and should define its own processes to suit its specific needs.

Procedures are the instructions that people follow to perform a process. These are the 'how to' guides. Where the process describes the steps, the procedures explain how to perform them. These are tied to organisation-specific processes and will usually be dependent on the tools used, as well as being dependent on the steps in the process.

Best practice frameworks provide an overarching guide to what should be included in a change management process that is tailored to your organisation's specific needs and operated consistently according to the procedures that support it.

This section introduces common relevant frameworks and links to further information.

ITIL®

ITIL® stands for IT Infrastructure Library, commonly known as ITIL®.

ITIL® is a widely accepted approach to ITSM, which has been adopted by individuals and organisations around the world. ITIL® provides a cohesive set of best practice, drawn from the public and private sectors internationally. Version 3 is set out in five core publications: *Service Strategy*, *Service Design*,

Service Transition, *Service Operation* and *Continual Service Improvement*. These five volumes map the entire ITIL Service Lifecycle, beginning with the identification of customer needs and drivers of IT requirements, moving through to the design and implementation of the service and, finally, the monitoring and improvement phase of the service.[6]

The change management process is defined in the *Service Transition* volume, but it has touchpoints throughout the lifecycle.

Version 4 is being launched in 2019. At the time of writing, the *Foundation* manual is hot off the press, with the full framework scheduled for later in the year.

ITIL® is mapped in ISO 20000.

COBIT®

COBIT® is a business framework for the governance and management of enterprise IT. It provides globally accepted principles, practices, analytical tools and models to help increase the trust in, and value from, information systems.[7]

Change management policies, processes and measures are included in COBIT®.

KEY POINTS

- Standards specify compulsory requirements that must all be met for compliance to be certified.
- Frameworks provide the collective wisdom of those experienced in the field.
- Processes and procedures are specific interpretations of standards or frameworks.

---

6 See www.axelos.com/best-practice-solutions/itil

7 See https://cobitonline.isaca.org/about

7 INTERFACES AND DEPENDENCIES

As is to be expected from such a pivotal role, the interfaces and dependencies for the change manager are many and varied.

The change manager will liaise with other roles in the organisation that are involved in the development and implementation of technical changes, including IT, business, customer and supplier representatives, limited only by the scope of technology deployment for which the change manager is responsible.

The change management process provides inputs to, and receives outputs from, other IT service management processes. Crucially, change management must adapt to work with whatever other methodologies are used to design, develop and implement changes, which themselves may be many and varied according to discipline, and packaged according to individual release life cycle, programme and project preferences.

Perhaps the greatest dependency for change management is the change culture that prevails in the organisation, which can make or break the success of the process. This chapter looks at each of these areas, starting with the overarching culture that is not always aligned with the intended direction of travel.

CHANGE CULTURE

A successful change management process cannot thrive in a culture of subversion. The establishment of the role of change manager suggests a desire to manage change, however new it may be. Unfortunately, the declaration alone is not usually enough to make it happen. As mentioned earlier, introducing change management when change is underway is almost certainly an attempt to persuade people to change their habits.

Resistant or not, old habits die hard anyway and in this case changing them usually involves spending more time up-front planning every change and recovering easily from occasional failed ones, rather than cutting corners for profit today in the hope of never getting caught tomorrow. Once a culture of instant gratification is established it can be very hard to reverse, especially if the perception is that everyone must change to suit the change manager.

In addition to that, resistance to change management is easily reinforced when the threat of business failure puts management reputations at risk and a change management process that is anything less than slick is abandoned for an any-fix-will-do-as-long-as-it-is-now approach. Every time this happens, the process is undermined and excuses for avoiding the process get weaker.

Unfortunately, in circumstances like these, the change manager can find themselves in a lose–lose situation. If they dig in their heels and demand that the process is followed whatever the situation, they will be seen as rigid and inflexible and worthy of ignoring. If they make even the slightest concession, they risk a stampede to trample on the process.

Chapter 4 includes tips on process implementation that are designed to encourage buy-in. The importance of consultation, management commitment, adopting current practices and building on them, and considering the needs of all participants in the context of their own ways of working cannot be understated, but culture change doesn't happen overnight, and perseverance is necessary in what can feel like interminable adversity at times.

In situations like this it pays to remember that continual improvement is more realistic than perfection. Be pragmatic;

know when to relax the rules; make your manager and your stakeholders your partners in compromise rather than adversaries in contention. Take every opportunity to review instances of difficulty for ways to improve the process for next time and be visible about it.

You can't hold back the tide single-handedly, but you can stand at the harbour and greet everyone as individuals. Don't hide behind rules and process excuses – or worse, refer them to your manager. The more up front you are with the courage of your convictions, the more and sooner the process will be taken seriously. Engagement rather than combat is the way forward.

Fresh starts only mean going over old ground so try to push through with minor concessions, not complete reversals. Above all, strive to make the process fit existing methods and life cycles, rather than make them fit your process. Remember that change management is a cog in the machine; on its own it's just a wheel with teeth.

WORKING WITH OTHER SERVICE MANAGEMENT PROCESSES

It has already been mentioned that change management is one part of a set of interlinked processes that together enable good practice management of IT services. This section aims to contextualise change management within service management by a simple overview. The five volumes of ITIL® provide a comprehensive source of detail about each of the processes and how they fit together in the lifecycle of IT services. Here, they are grouped according to their relationship with change: as sources of change, contributors to change and consequences of change; as a way of describing the inputs, the actors and the outputs of change management in the language of service management.

Sources of change

Change can be the output of other processes and functions. This section describes how this might happen.

Problem management

Problem management is a source of change that fixes problems. The process might be formalised through a problem manager, or it might be an extension of service desk, second line support and incident management, third line support, or all of the above. Although ITIL® defines problem management as separate from incident management, in practice incidents often lead directly to permanent fixes (as opposed to temporary workarounds). Arguably, this makes them problems, by definition, but they may not be identified separately.

Problem management can also be deployed as a separate function that reviews incidents to look for trends and underlying issues that are not causing immediate trouble to service users. This might lead to changes that can be scheduled comfortably in accordance with normal change management review and approval cycles, as opposed to changes identified as a direct result of incidents that might need a more aggressive reactive response. These might trigger the emergency change process, depending on the impact of the incident and local interpretation of the process. A separate major incidents process could determine how they are handled.

Event management

Event management monitors services for performance threshold triggers and potential component failures. This, too, might result in proactive or reactive changes, whether or not they go through an incident or problem management process first.

Release and deployment management

The process of release and deployment management is good friends with change management. Structured planning and development of new and upgraded applications and other software, often into predetermined release packages and schedules, make it easy for change management to mesh with its practices and lifecycles. With no formal release and deployment management process, new software and upgrades are just more changes that need to be assessed for impact and risk and planned and implemented accordingly.

With a formal process, the change management job is half done but it must go halfway to meet it to avoid unnecessary rework.

Continual service improvement

Continual service improvement is the systematic review of, and reflection on, performance, process and lessons learned across the IT domain, not just in change management. Like problem trend analysis, continual service improvement can identify changes that will lead to improvements in performance, reliability, resilience or just plain usability. As a strategic process, it should generate changes that can be planned and implemented using the change management process.

Contributors to change

Other processes that can stand alone might also participate directly in the change management process.

Service validation and testing

Service validation and testing is another ITIL® process, but it is more likely to make its entrance in change management on the back of release and deployment. Commonly associated with software quality assurance, there is no reason why its principles cannot be used to describe how to assure the quality of any change. Furthermore, existing testing processes should be embedded in the change management process, not reinvented for duplication of effort. The test plan in a request for change can refer out to the pre-existing process, provided it is transparent.

Evaluation

Evaluation is fundamental to deciding whether a change gets the go-ahead for development. Team and managerial hierarchies can undermine the full benefit of change management, by making a change a foregone conclusion before it enters the process. Evaluation may have taken place before a change is assigned for development, or it may have been slipped in on assumption, but, in any case, it runs the risk of being assessed in isolation. Viewed from within the process, by the change manager, reviewers, approvers and CAB members, a proposal is illuminated in the context of the master plan. Evaluation of change viability within the process might make the process look longer and (even) more time-consuming, but it takes place somewhere, so why not formalise it and eliminate assumptions? For the sake of pragmatism, in a resistant climate, it is a concession that might be introduced later as a process adjustment, once the benefits of change management for implementation alone have been sold.

Processes such as security management, availability management, and capacity and demand management should contribute to the evaluation of changes at every stage and should be key considerations before anything is decided. They all need to be built in or made adequate to accommodate change, and review and approval are required from all of their representatives.

Service level management

Service level management contributes to change management at both ends. When planning, forethought should determine the agreement of maintenance time for IT systems and ideally it will be possible to agree slots with the business when everyone (else) is sleeping. This makes approving changes that fall into this category easier, provided the change planners stick to the agreed windows of opportunity. If convenient times can be agreed at the service level agreement stage, there is no need to keep asking for permission to implement maintenance changes (but it is always nice to know when they are being taken up).

At the implementation end, service level managers will want some assurance that changes proposed will not affect agreed service availability, and their caution, or otherwise, will be dictated by the degree of penalty to be inflicted by the customer in the event of breach. Service level managers are key players in the approval of changes, should play an active role in change advisory board meetings and will almost certainly show a keen interest in reports that show the impact of change on services.

Consequences of change

Finally, changes become outputs directly relevant to other processes and functions, and, in some cases, control their content.

Configuration management

Changes are the consequence of change. If you have a configuration management system or database, it should mirror reality. If something is changed in the configuration, as the result of the successful implementation of an approved request for change, the configuration management system must be updated immediately as a consequence, so that downstream planners are working with the correct assumptions.

The change manager will need to work with the configuration manager to agree a process for updating records. Change implementers may not automatically assume it is their job to dot the i's and cross the t's, and appropriate access to records will need to be granted to those authorised. It doesn't matter who does it, provided that someone does, but the change manager must ensure that it is agreed and facilitated, because this is an output of change management that requires handshake acceptance.

Grow your own CMS

There is a lot to be done in the planning for a configuration management system and this is not the place to document it. But there is a critical path that puts an effective change management process directly in front of populating a CMS that is assured to be accurate. If you gather your CMS data in isolation, a change is almost certain to come along while you are doing it – to make your data out of date before you've even got it into the system.

You need the change management process as the funnel through which all configuration data goes. One way of building a CMS organically is to make the data-gathering exercise part of the initial change planning in the request for change. After all, you can't do an effective impact and risk assessment if you don't know what it is you are changing and, anyway, why would you be planning a change to something unspecified? The data is needed to effectively plan and implement the change and can be squirted out of the change process at the other end in its modified form, straight into the empty CMS. No time lag, no inaccuracies.

An attraction of this approach is that the CMS is created as a by-product of change management. By breaking the data gathering down into small manageable chunks, it is distributed naturally as part of work already planned and the danger of it being out of date by the time the change is complete is removed. The downside is that it could take forever to complete, and verification is an important additional step at the start because any locally stored information (or knowledge in people's heads) should be validated as accurate. But it depends on priorities and, as a small-scale start-up approach, it conveys the dependence of the CMS on change management to all involved (and should result in a light bulb moment on how unauthorised change can be identified).

Knowledge management

Knowledge management could be centralised, loosely linked in a deliberately federated system, distributed, fragmented, incomplete or non-existent. Arguably, a knowledge management system is integral to the configuration management system and as such should be updated with the relevant outputs of the change management process. In practice, it might be a separate output from a project, but it should nevertheless be acknowledged in a request for change.

161

Knowledge could be anything from procedures for installation to support tips for the service desk, and there is a degree of overlap with other processes. Service portfolios and service catalogues will change if services change, and the delivery of services in accordance with service level agreements might be affected. IT service continuity plans will look a bit silly if they invoke the replication of an old version because they didn't know there was a new one and business continuity plans are meaningless if they are not kept up to date.

Service desk

Last, but certainly not least, the service desk is a function not a process, but it still needs to be there when the loop is closed. As the single point of contact in IT they must be knowledgeable about anything they are asked.

WORKING WITH OTHER METHODS AND APPROACHES

Change management should not be at odds with other methods and approaches. The change manager should work with representatives to integrate change management in a way that is effective for the business. This means aligning the request for change cycle with project management and embedding change management requirements into Agile approaches to delivering business benefit that is faster than traditional methods.

The change manager should focus on harnessing the evidence of internal change management and maintaining centralised data for visibility and accurate reporting, rather than building in the repetition of change management measures already established and extending the process unnecessarily.

Project management

Projects inside IT might be IT specific, such as a project to upgrade all routers, or fileservers or operating systems; or they might be business-area specific, such as business process digital transformation projects or upgrades driven by business requirements.

Like release management, projects usually already consider many of the aspects of good practice technical change management within project management and the change manager can and should work with this to avoid too much overlap in the effort required across the two processes. In PRINCE2®[1] (the project management method) for example, standard concepts include a business case, plans, controls, continual management of risks, quality assurance, change controls and configuration management.

Unlike release management, projects are likely to be one-off events, or a programme of related events, that do not fit into a repeatable release schedule or consistent approach. The change manager will need to work closely with project managers from an early stage so that they can help with the timing of requests for change and bring in, or advise on, ad hoc reviewers and approvers. The change manager shouldn't need to vary the change management process to fit a project but will need to guide a project through so that critical paths converge.

If project managers understand the requirements of the change management process, it should be possible for them to build a request for technical change alongside the initiation and development of a project. A business case should be required before a project is approved for development, so it follows that the reason for technical change has an identifiable source early in the process. Approval to proceed with technical change can therefore be aligned with project approval.

Planning and controls established once should be good enough to satisfy the technical change process when technical change is integral to a project. Continual risk management is better than a once-only exercise anyway, and the concept of inspecting outcomes against standards in quality assurance is testing by any other name. Considering that control of change to a project's requirements and scope, and the idea of planning against an existing configuration, are already anticipated elements of project

---

1   See www.axelos.com/best-practice-solutions/prince2

management it should not be difficult to extract the relevant evidences, such as impact assessment and priority, to satisfy the central overview and management of technical change.

The project manager must respect the importance of the central view and, of course, should be working from the same configuration management system as the change manager, but the change manager, equally, should respect the discipline already embedded in the project management methods. Working together to establish the synergies and boundaries should result in a lean process where project managers are left to manage their projects but change management touchpoints are transferred to the change manager for appropriate dissemination. The CAB should want to acknowledge project changes viewed alongside other changes to be able to ratify schedules, since projects do not happen in isolation and the world does not revolve around any one activity. The central view still belongs to the change manager.

Software development

Traditional software development methods such as the waterfall approach fit well with change management. They follow a linear path that involves defining requirements, developing products and testing them as sequential steps carried out over time, which can be aligned comfortably with change management cycles. In this context, the demands of the change process can generally be comfortably absorbed into the planning stages without becoming too onerous.

However, Agile approaches such as Scrum[2] and DevOps[3] work on the principle of 'release early, release often',[4] with fast iterations of design, development, testing and refinement of minimum viable products.[5] Agile approaches were invented,

---

[2] See www.scrumalliance.org/

[3] See www.oreilly.com/ideas/the-evolution-of-devops

[4] See https://en.wikipedia.org/wiki/Release_early,_release_often

[5] See https://en.wikipedia.org/wiki/Minimum_viable_product

at least in part, out of a need to be more responsive to business timescales and some might argue that the perceived bureaucracy of change management was a trigger. Certainly, the potential for change management to be at cross purposes with a lean and modular approach warrants specific attention for the change manager.

While the fast pace of self-governed Agile methods might seem to be at odds with an overarching change management process, it is important that the baby should not go out with the bathwater, and the principles of change management must be embedded at an appropriately granular level within the development cycle. To make it work, Agile teams must own their change management and demonstrate their adherence to change policy. And that's really the point. It is not that Agile teams are maverick, resisting control, but that they are already positioned to understand the impact of their actions and minimise adverse impact on the business directly and dynamically through the continual integration of change.

In this case the change manager's role could be to set out the policy and requirements and provide the tools, with the configuration manager, that enable development teams to manage their own change within the parameters set. Provided that they can demonstrate this, the change manager can disseminate what has been done to ensure transparency between processes. Development teams are not exempt from the process and should participate in CAB meetings as required but should not have to demonstrate their compliance twice because the first process was 'not invented here'. In this way ownership of change is where it should be, rather than with the change manager.

It is a contradiction in terms to expect a self-governed Agile method to wait for management approval via an external process, and bolting a redundant process on the end of an existing one defeats the object of the Agile approach. But Agile methods must accept the responsibility to conform with the requirements of change management (as opposed to necessarily following the process). As with project managers, the change manager should work with development teams to help them meet the needs of change management in a way that justifies exemption from a separate process. And the development teams must respect the change manager's position as well. They are entitled to do things their way and the change manager is entitled to enforce change management.

In an ideal world, the change manager will coordinate multiple devolved and distributed change management processes according to discipline and development methods. Change management as a top-down process came into being out of the need for systematic impact and risk management in multiple environments where none existed in the early days of IT service provision. Robust methodologies now require a relinquishing of control back to those who can do it best.

However, conflict can arise from competing processes and how the change manager responds will vary depending on departmental capability. If change management principles can sensibly be embedded in native processes, the change manager should encourage and facilitate this; but the change management process is the default position in the absence of effective autonomy. The outcomes should be the same. The goal is for all to play nicely.

WORKING WITH OTHER IT ROLES

The change manager will work with a wide range of roles spread across IT. The roles suggested are hypothetical roles, like the change manager role. An individual organisation might adopt different job titles and assign roles according to need. The descriptions here are generic but give a flavour of scope.

The change manager will have direct contact with the person creating requests for change. That could be someone in a software or infrastructure team, a project manager, programme manager or problem manager. It could be someone in the same organisation or someone in a supplier organisation. It might be another change manager, depending on the context.

The change manager will liaise with representatives from departments and teams affected by changes and with those who will have a view on the impact of changes. These might be an information security manager, a service level manager, a business relationship manager, or anyone representing the interests of affected parts of the configuration, from applications to capacity, data storage to maintenance windows.

The service desk manager will be a key contact. They should be involved in approvals and scheduling, because they will need to ensure that appropriate resourcing is in place according to risk and timetable. They will want to know the outcome of changes promptly, so they can respond accordingly to callers and they will report any detected or perceived adverse effects of change to the change manager for investigation.

The configuration manager will be a partner in identifying unauthorised changes manifest in alterations to the configuration management system that bypassed the change management process, if a configuration management system exists. This is potentially the biggest black hole that the change manager might face – the ability to validate risk and impact assessments against available and accurate information. There is an inherent risk in accepting at face value a request for a change author's account of impact and risk if it cannot be independently verified. Peer review is essential if source information is questionable.

Peer reviewers and approvers are the change manager's friends. The change manager is only responsible for the process, not the decisions made in its operation. That load is shared with the author, reviewers and approvers, based on collective responsibility for the content and its analysis. The change manager is responsible for facilitating the decision through the best representation of the facts, assumptions and preparation to reach the desired outcome.

Mitigation, not guarantee

Having a change management process and a change manager doesn't guarantee problem-free change. The change management process can only mitigate against risks that are foreseeable or hypothesised; it can't legislate for the unknowable. Change management is about taking as much control as possible to reduce the likelihood of problems resulting from change. Risks are managed; you can't eliminate them entirely or make assumptions from experience.

Working with reviewers and approvers means guarding against complacency. The change manager must ask the right questions to be assured that due consideration has been given; that risk and impact have been thought about, not just copied and pasted from another request for change. When the process of review and approval becomes a box-ticking exercise, the change management process is no longer doing something useful, it is just a job creation scheme.

WORKING WITH SUPPLIERS AND SERVICE PROVIDERS

Suppliers and service providers will need to be dealt with on a case-by-case basis, depending on what they do and how they do it. A supplier might provide telecoms solutions with infrastructure onsite, for example. In circumstances such as this, it is fairly clear-cut that to gain access to make changes some checks should be expected before access is granted. It is reasonable to expect suppliers to work with their customer's supplier manager or other suitably skilled contact at the customer site, who will translate their plans into the host change management process. It is also reasonable to expect that the supplier's own governance extends to the appropriate management of change planning at their end, but it should not be necessary or desirable for a customer change manager to be directly involved in this. In this respect, the manager responsible for the supplier relationship should be a regular contact and informant for the change manager and they might have a regular seat on the change advisory board to represent their third parties.

On the other hand, service providers represent a greyer area, and much will depend on the service architecture and how personal the relationship is with the customer. Providers of generic services such as productivity tools and cloud storage will likely please themselves and state their case in pre-emptive terms and conditions. You fire up your machine; you take your chance. It might be just another productive day, or it might be undermined by unexpected functionality changes (ironically, an aspect of change that presaged good practice change management that now appears to be bathwater on its way out with the baby). Negotiated services should bring with them some agreement on the process for change. Ideally that will also be specified up front, in the form of service level agreements with agreed maintenance windows, but there should be some mechanism for feeding into the customer change management process for anything outside that framework, and notification is always helpful for planning and diagnostic purposes. As costs are likely to be involved in whatever this turns out to be, it will be part of the procurement process, which should relate the needs directly to business criticality. The change manager will be led by this and work with their colleague supplier managers to establish protocol.

WORKING WITH OTHER BUSINESS ROLES

When technical change is driven by business change, it seems logical that there is a process for business change that should dictate the process for technical change. The business change process shouldn't have to jump through hoops to please technical change, but technical change is a specialist sub-set of the wider change picture and should nevertheless be thorough.

The IT change manager should build good relationships with business change and digital transformation managers, whether they exist in dedicated jobs or whether they are allocated programme and project managers according to need. The difference here is the emphasis on the impact on people and the role of business change in transforming behaviours, as well as delivering new processes and tools.

Apart from the now common theme of enabling self-managed change to avoid duplication of effort and speed up the process of technical change, here the change manager also needs to work within the parameters of wider business change management, especially in terms of communication. Business change managers should have the final say on the publication of change schedules so that they can coordinate the announcement of technical change with their own message if necessary or desirable. The technical change manager must be mindful of the sensitivities of business change and operate under direction as required. They should approach business change managers to establish their needs early and support them in getting business change right.

WORKING WITH CUSTOMERS

Last, but not least, without the customer there is no change or change management. The customer is the ultimate interface and dependency, whether they are internal service users or external purchasers.

Change management is an easy target for blame when it is perceived to interfere with, delay or block change, even if it was only introduced in the first place to limit the negative impacts on end-users. Good or bad, the customer has the final say, whether it is formally or informally. It is the customer's risk to take and if they perceive the benefits to outweigh the risks and want change now, the change manager may be overridden. Alternatively, it is the prerogative of the customer to take their custom elsewhere.

The change manager must maintain the message on the benefits of fit-for-purpose change management and keep it fit for purpose – no more, no less. Essentially, the change management process should be invisible to customers, but the benefits, articulated regularly by the change manager, should be kept in the forefronts of their minds. If the message becomes out of sight and out of mind, taking the benefits for granted could be the slippery slope back to the bad old days of anarchic change.

The change management process should be in a constant state of flux, as different parts of the organisation take up and let out slack in the process of change. The change manager maintains appropriate tension by flexing in response. Result: a taut and responsive risk management service.

KEY POINTS

- The change manager works with roles across IT, the business, customers and suppliers.

- Processes either side of change management need to be in place in some form or other, however formal or informal they may be.

- But the world should not be expected to revolve around the change management process; rather, the change management process should be an extension of working practices where these exist already.

8 CAREER PROGRESSION AND RELATED ROLES

It should be easy by now to see that routes into change management can come from many directions, and the roads out are just as varied. There are no limits, but this chapter provides some of the more obvious options, along with ideas on qualifications to support you on the journey.

BECOMING A CHANGE MANAGER

There is no fixed way of becoming a change manager. The change manager is an all-rounder, with a technical bent but a feel for business and an affinity with flux.

Depending on the size of an organisation, and its throughput of change, there might be opportunities to begin as a change analyst, supporting a change manager. SFIA*plus* describes the activities at lower levels of change management, including the skills required.[1] Anyone with a blend of technical and customer-facing skills in a current IT role could be a suitable candidate, but the role of business analyst might be the closest in skill set, with its emphasis on technical and business focus in equal measure, and proximity to technical change.

Because the extent of the change manager role reaches across the spectrum of the business, it is equally possible to enter from outside IT. However, there is perhaps a greater requirement for empathy with the workings of IT teams

---

[1] https://bit.ly/30vEC9q (BCS members only) or http://www.bcs.org/sfiaplus (non-members)

than business teams as they are the sources of technical change and information: the inputs. See **Chapter 2** for more information on how technical it is necessary to be.

Understanding the process is a key requirement. The blossoming change manager might come from a technical team familiar with the change process through direct participation, or they may be on the fringes of it. Reading ITIL® or COBIT® will provide the theory, but some understanding of its application is desirable since it is an abstract concept on paper. Good qualifications can simulate the process and could be a useful addition where direct experience is lacking.

Opportunities, and salaries, can vary. Search for 'change manager' or 'change analyst' on job portals and talk to recruitment agencies to look for vacancies and get a feel for what is current.

Chapter 2 describes the roles and responsibilities, knowledge, skills and behaviours of the change manager and the portrait of a change manager described there should help to identify aptitudes.

Qualifications

Specialist certificates available to support change managers include offerings under the ITIL® and BCS suites of service management qualifications.

At the time of writing, ITIL® has various routes through its qualification framework, including different aspects of change management, at five levels: Foundation, Practitioner, Intermediate, Expert and Master. Foundation level introduces all the ITIL® processes and is a pre-requisite for subsequent levels. Choices at Intermediate level can be tailored to suit individual needs and the training navigator tool helps to plan this. Full details can be found on the Axelos website.[2]

---

2   See www.axelos.com/certifications/itil-certifications

BCS qualifications take a similar approach. The overarching service management VeriSM™ model contains a series of specialist certificates, including change management. These embrace service management best practice frameworks, including ITIL®, COBIT®, ISO/IEC 20000 and SFIA/SFIA*plus*, amongst others. Full details can be found on the BCS website under professional certification, IT service and asset management.[3]

Are qualifications necessary?

It is perfectly reasonable to be able to learn and perform the role of change manager without taking a specialist qualification. Reading the many resources available, immersion in the job and shadowing role models are all good ways to learn. Learning on the job trumps facts that have not been applied and if it is a choice between experience and a qualification, experience is more useful in the short and long term.

But qualifications often play an important role in the recruitment process for newcomers to an organisation and may be specified as minimum requirements, however experienced an applicant might be. The prevailing market conditions will drive entry-level requirements but gaining qualifications as well as experience can only be advantageous.

Continuing professional development

Continuing professional development, or CPD, is essential if you are to stay up to date in any role. Good practice evolves, new standards and obligations emerge, qualifications are updated and lessons learned. Standing still is not an option

---

3 See https://certifications.bcs.org/category/15413

and this is never truer than in a field where change is intrinsic to its operation. Managing your continuing professional development is a sign that you take your role seriously and staying current will help you to stay marketable when you want to change jobs.

Taking initial qualifications might represent CPD for those not yet qualified but there are other opportunities, often linked to membership of professional bodies. Evidence of CPD can often be a requirement of membership and professional bodies may produce guidance on how much is recommended and on the value of the opportunities they offer.

BCS[4] is The Chartered Institute for IT and a membership organisation for those in related fields. Members benefit from a range of services and tools for career development, including CPD guidance and resources. Its SFIA**plus** tool provides specific suggestions for change management CPD.

The itSMF (IT Service Management Forum) has UK[5] and international[6] chapters and is a membership organisation for IT service management professionals, including change managers. It, too, provides a range of opportunities for professional development such as conferences, workshops and special interest groups.

The Change Management Body of Knowledge[7] (CMBoK) describes the Change Management Institute Change Manager Competency Model[8] and the competencies required to deliver change successfully. The Change Management Institute[9] offers membership benefits for change management professionals.

---

4   See www.bcs.org/

5   See www.itsmf.co.uk/

6   See www.itsmfi.org/

7   See www.change-management-institute.com/buycmbok

8   See www.change-management-institute.com/competency-model

9   See www.change-management-institute.com/

Understanding and developing into the broader organisational change management remit might be a natural progression and mapping synergies between the types of change management is a good place to start. Topics such as impact assessment, planning, project management and communication all play significant roles in organisational change and the technical change manager has a foundation in these subjects on which to build.

It may also be worth considering university or commercial[10] courses in organisational behaviour, leadership and management to help bridge between technical and organisation change management disciplines.

BEYOND THE ROLE OF CHANGE MANAGER

As already stated, many of the skills of the technical change manager are transferable into the wider field of organisational change, and experience on the cusp of IT and business demonstrates exposure to the bigger picture and a grasp of the sources of change.

In fact, the transferable skills in technical change management underpin many other IT and non-IT roles. Communication skills, project management, managing stakeholder relationships and general facilitation skills are generic enough to apply to any number of managerial and other roles.

If progressing from business analyst to change manager is a viable route then the reverse must also be true, with the development of the corresponding specialist skills that this entails. A change manager stepping into project or programme manager roles would bring not just the transferable skills, but also a comprehensive understanding of, and sympathy with, the change management process and a head start in working the system.

---

[10] See www.i-l-m.com/learning-and-development/leadership-and-management-qualifications

Permanent employment could lead to temporary assignments in the same role but in other companies, the ultimate in flexibility for the change-obsessed change manager who likes to mix it up to the max. Interim roles can be rewarding, especially when they involve embedding a new process. Some people thrive on bringing old experience to new situations; for others this is akin to the punishment of Sisyphus, condemned repeatedly to push the boulder almost to the top of the hill before it rolls back to the bottom.[11] In any case, it is wise to consult the market before taking the plunge, as opportunities, and rates, can vary. Search for 'change manager' on job portals and talk to recruitment agencies.

Change and service management tool providers and software companies could be a good option for the change manager who wants to focus on process automation, with a range of possible opportunities from pre-sales to configuration consultancy. Consultancy in general could beckon – sharing expertise with those at the start of the change management journey, as a freelancer or working for a larger consultancy. As with interim roles, opportunities in the freelance market vary.

Beware the magic bullet

Clients will hire you to make use of your expertise and experience and may see this as a shortcut to getting the process right first time. But remember that what you have learned is based on what you have done. New contexts are new challenges and local culture must be acknowledged and respected. It is unlikely, in reality, that clients will be able to learn from your mistakes but guiding them through theirs can be helpful.

Setting expectations is important and first attempts at process implementation can be the first of many. They

---

11 www.britannica.com/topic/Sisyphus

are valuable because they inform the learning process. Try to help your clients see this as a positive outcome. Your contribution will help to steer them in the right direction, but some trial and error is inevitable because every organisation is different. There is no shortcut or magic bullet.

Everywhere is different, just applying the same concepts to create their own current version of good practice. Remember, the only thing that is constant is change.

KEY POINTS

- There are many transferable skills attributable to a change manager.

- Qualifications can give an experienced change manager the edge.

- The world is your oyster!

9   CASE STUDIES

The case studies in this chapter form a hypothetical account of three different levels of maturity for the role of technical change manager. They are snapshots along a continuum of endless possibilities for variation and are intended to show that change management is not all or nothing but a continual work in progress, and some is better than none. The aim here is to pull together exemplars of some of the topics discussed in this guide, breathing life into the words.

All are fictional, created with inspiration from a blend of personal experience – both inside and outside change management – observations, consultation and optimism. Any resemblance to actual persons, events or circumstances is purely coincidental.

THE IDEAL CHANGE MANAGER

The ideal change manager represents a relatively stable approach to change management that is widely accepted; processes and tools are mature, and everyone is travelling in the same direction. The relative maturity of this role is something to aspire to.

Business and IT context

The ideal change manager works for Company A, a multinational with regional headquarters in the UK, Southeast Asia and the USA. All three sites are operational; there is also a large research and development division on the UK campus.

Each regional HQ provides IT services to satellite offices. There is a service desk at each HQ, which provides additional out-of-hours support for business users across time zones, and each site has a data centre serving its region and hosting all regional services. The site configurations mirror each other to the extent that service continuity plans could be invoked quickly in the event of a major incident at any site.

The technology underpinning core services is developed internally for the group, mostly in Southeast Asia but with some development in the UK and the USA for local requirements. There is a large development team that must respond to market changes and put in fixes quickly to prevent costly business downtime. They use a DevOps-style approach that has evolved from experimenting with Agile software development approaches.

Each region has applications local to them in addition to the core shared services, and local suppliers are used. Office systems are outsourced to subscription services.

Background to change management

Change management is well established, with state-of-the-art tools. There is a change manager at each regional HQ and they have collaborated well over time to find ways of working together and ensure appropriate communication across all sites. It has taken a while to get the different plates spinning all at once, but it has been worth the effort. The change management process is acknowledged as beneficial and custom approaches to different areas ensure that it is not hindering the business, which had been a fault commonly perceived in the earlier stages.

Much of the process is now effectively automated and the change managers are free to focus on the one-offs and emergencies that can represent greater risk to the business for their uniqueness. They are not bogged down in repetitive work; everyone is free to develop and improve further. They also accept that change will keep affecting the process and they are ready to respond when that happens.

Process

As far as company-wide change is concerned, operational change types are roughly divided into three areas: application development, infrastructure maintenance and infrastructure growth.

Initially, the application development methodology fed into a separate release process tied to change management, but this caused some frustration for the development team, and the business, who felt they were not realising the benefits of a fully Agile approach and writing lengthy requests for change was at odds with the Agile concept.

The change manager in Southeast Asia sat down with representatives from development there to discuss methods and look for overlap that could reduce the need for rework in change management. They found that the heavy reliance on testing in the development stage provided natural mitigation and they were also discussing risk and impact in their fortnightly sprint planning meetings. Product owners were directly involved and were prepared to make the call on whether the risk was greater in proceeding or not proceeding, according to the business position.

To capitalise on these aspects, a 'request for change lite' was embedded at the start of the development sprint and to mitigate further they agreed with the UK change manager and developers to trial deployments first in the UK, where there was the least business impact. This would be a 'live' test, so that decisions could be taken to roll-out to Southeast Asia and the USA based on what happened in the UK first. The UK site is the smallest and it is easiest to back out the change there, if necessary, with limited impact on the business.

This has resulted in a standard 'fast-track' approach tailored to the cross-site development process, which is largely independent of the core change management cycle. Requests for change are effectively approved at the development planning meetings. The respective change manager attends these meetings and updates the CAB agenda and change schedule for information only. In exceptional circumstances a change manager might request a development team representative to attend the local CAB to explain further what is happening, but this is the exception rather than the rule.

The same idea has been taken a step further in the UK, where the company's large Research & Development (R&D) division is located. The work done here is separate from the operational day-to-day work, but, of course, is important to its future success. The tools used here evolve with the research work, and change must be dynamic to avoid costly lost time, even though the pipeline to operational has a much longer lifecycle. However, R&D is self-contained and what it does has no direct impact on the operational infrastructure, so with some up-front mitigation and some ground-rules agreed and in place, they have full control 'outside' change management. A dedicated IT team manages the infrastructure, with agreed maintenance windows. For any other essential work, there is an agreed communications plan to make sure everyone affected by the change knows the schedule and is empowered to raise an objection that will be discussed through the change manager. The back-up process has been verified and restores are tested regularly as a condition of the exemption. The ability to recover from a change is proven and rehearsed as a service continuity approach. This is the safety net that allows changes to be made without further approval.

Engagement with change management, for communication and reporting about these types of changes, is through standard fast-track changes that are completed in the change management system but require no further approval. As with development, changes appear on the CAB agenda and change schedule for information. Risk management is reviewed monthly by IT and business representatives from R&D with the UK change manager, in the light of changes made, and the process is reviewed for continued suitability. The full change management process can be reintroduced at any time if necessary.

Across the three sites, each change manager has agreed other fast-track changes for repeated maintenance activities. Like R&D, these must be scheduled to take place in agreed maintenance windows to qualify for information-only presentation, otherwise they are treated as new changes and must go through the full review and approval cycle.

Everything else is assumed to be ad hoc or related to projects and processed to align with weekly CAB meetings, with representatives of changes attending to share updates and answer questions. Suppliers are not permitted to make changes directly without CAB approval and they will be represented by respective Company A supplier managers.

CAB

Each change manager holds a local CAB meeting every Tuesday, which is attended by appropriate technical and business representation. The three change managers then hold a virtual meeting every Wednesday at noon GMT, to update each other, and this meeting is known by the team as the 'CAB summit'. This is an early start for the US change manager, and a late finish in Southeast Asia, but it is the best time-zone compromise and they have found that a short 'face-to-face' meeting using web conferencing is more effective than trying to discuss post-implementation reviews and plans for the forthcoming week just by sharing documents and emailing or messaging each other.

To begin with they had tried virtual attendance at each other's local CAB meetings, but it took up a whole day for each of them and gave them little time to catch up on the admin quickly after their own meetings, when it was important to update status on changes going in the same day. It was a long day with no slack for unplanned events. Also, although there were commonalities in many of the changes across the three regions, there were also local-only subjects that were not relevant to the other two managers. They had tried sticking to a strictly organised agenda to compartmentalise their attendance but in the end decided it was more important to give free reign to the local technical and business representatives involved in CAB decisions than to share across the three sites at the same time, and so the CAB summit was born and has worked effectively ever since.

Tools

The company is now using a top-of-the-range, software-as-a-service integrated IT service management system for service desk, incident management and self-service; service level management; problem management; change management; and configuration management. The sites use the same product, but in local instances. The change management process is configured to be the same across the three locations, with the same core data sets for common reporting, done by a dedicated analyst at each site. Each has its own configuration management system to enable flexibility and maximise manageability. This has allowed each HQ to specify its own configuration item and attribute sets to suit local resources and requirements, some of which are compliance-related, without the others becoming cluttered with unused fields.

The development of the configuration management system had a few false starts. In hindsight, those responsible can see that, to begin with, they were too ambitious in trying to build a one-size-fits-all system across the global network. With so many people involved in specifying requirements, they became entrenched in discussions and ended up with an over-engineered set of data requirements that they couldn't hope to gather and maintain, even with a good change management process already in place. Breaking it down by site had the effect of speeding up three separate projects to earlier delivery, and the prior experience taught everyone that just because you can record something, it doesn't mean you should! Now the CMS is routinely used to plan changes and the change process closes the loop by making sure records are updated when changes are complete. It is relied upon and assumed to be reliable, because everyone knows that regular verification audits take place. This alone has improved the change management process by removing a lot of head-scratching in impact assessments.

This is the company's third service management tool, the first being limited to incident logging and some asset management and the second being their first implementation of an integrated system. The integrated system was a comprehensive tool, installed at each site and hosted fully by them. They underwent a thorough consultancy process, but they only fully understood what they really needed as they started to use it, which in hindsight was inevitable, regardless of how much discussion and agreement takes place in advance. It had been configured by the supplier consultant and they were responsive to changes, but they hadn't factored in the extra cost, so they had been limited in approval to make changes.

Now, some years later, the value of the system is proven, and processes have matured. Approval was sought to upgrade, and they decided at the same time to adopt software-as-a-service and train administrators for each site, so they could manage their own configuration (and reconfiguration!). An anticipated benefit of the new system was dynamic software updates applied remotely, and they took advantage of the modular approach by buying just the processes currently in use, with an option to add on as required. This option was available for their existing tool as well, and they considered the benefits of continuing to own the system outright; they had been very happy with the reporting tools, but in the end felt that it was a good time to look at new approaches. In the early days, they viewed mistakes as failures but have come to value the learning curve and now see themselves aligned with Agile approaches to development – in change management, and as a company. Furthermore, they now have a lot of experience behind them that will inform the design of the new system, so the risks are lowered.

The ideal change manager's ideal week

This ideal change manager works for the UK division of Company A and represents the change management process for the region and at a global level with the change managers at the other HQ sites. An ideal week provides a mix of regular and ad hoc activities, with quieter periods and inevitable responsibilities outside normal working hours.

Monday

Monday is an early start, to check on the outcome of changes implemented over the weekend. There had been some routine firmware upgrades on routers on Friday night and an application update from development in Southeast Asia on Sunday. There had been no calls at the weekend to report any issues on the firmware upgrade and the Southeast Asia team had confirmed successful deployment on Sunday afternoon. However, the first users on Monday should flush out any usage issues so it was important to be there early to pick up any problems that might prevent cascade to the other HQ sites. An early check-in with the service desk confirmed nothing to report so far and made them aware of the change manager's presence and interest should anything come in later.

Next is a review of the change management system to look at the status and outcomes of the weekend changes in detail. Updates to the CMS are checked – it is vital that these are processed immediately following a change so that any new changes being planned are done so on accurate information. The firmware upgrade was reported as incomplete. Some routers were successfully updated but the implementation team had to stop work in time to test that functionality was restored, so that the preparation and deployment of the application change from Southeast Asia could go ahead as planned.

The request for change for the application change has been updated with details of its success, but the post-implementation review has been left open for now to see how things go during Monday. Following the system check the change manager sits down with their line manager for a brief morning update. It is expected that confirmation to go ahead with the application cascade to Southeast Asia and the USA will be confirmed at the end of the day.

Tomorrow is the local CAB meeting, so it is important to check progress on the detail of the requests for change to be discussed. The agenda is generated from the change management system and the first view was made available to attendees last Thursday. However, it is common practice for updates to be applied up to a cut-off of 1 p.m. the day before the meeting, so that information is up to date and line approvals are in place where possible. Ideally, the CAB is an exercise in ratification for most changes. A few calls are made to chase up the inputs.

There are some routine queries from various implementation and project teams about forthcoming pieces of work and the change manager advises accordingly. They are working on some improvements to Frequently Asked Questions on the company intranet pages for UK change management and arranging some briefings. There has been an increase in employment of contract staff in project areas and although change management training is part of the induction for employees and contractors, it has proved beneficial in the past to take a direct interest and set out the process requirements in context. It is extra work up front but the time is well invested as in the longer term there are fewer ad hoc questions, which seemed to come in repeatedly in the past.

Mid-afternoon, the change manager receives a call from the implementation lead for the router firmware upgrade that took place on Friday. They would like to complete the outstanding routers over the forthcoming weekend, if this doesn't clash with other work, but realise they have missed the deadline for this week's CAB agenda. The change manager checks the expected plans and suggests that Sunday might be a possibility, after some server maintenance work in the pipeline for Saturday. The implementation lead agrees to attend the CAB meeting on Tuesday in exchange for leaving the open request for change on the agenda to be revisited at the meeting. As it was just a matter of running out of time to finish the updates on all routers it shouldn't be a problem, but attendance at the meeting will give approvers a chance to ask questions for reassurance and confirm that the short notice is acceptable to business plans.

After this discussion the change manager updates the CAB agenda and pushes a message out to all attendees to notify them of the change in advance of the meeting. There are no changes for implementation on Monday night and after a quick further check with the service desk, the change manager confirms that the application upgrade post-implementation review can be completed and lets the change managers in Southeast Asia and the USA know that they can confirm the cascade at their own CAB meetings the next day.

Tuesday

Tuesday is CAB day. The meeting starts at 10 a.m. and is scheduled to last for two hours. Actual length varies according to agenda; sometimes it finishes early and, if it is imperative, the meeting will overrun to keep changes on track, but this is avoided as far as possible to prevent disruption to the plans of others.

The change manager chairs the meeting and updates requests for change as decisions are made during the meeting. This is straightforward for changes in status, time and brief comments, and doesn't take up too much time. If discussions become lengthy and there is a need to record the decision-making process for future reference, notes are taken and typed directly into a document by the service desk representative. What needs to be recorded is usually directed by the change manager, but having someone to write things down during proceedings prevents lengthy delays while the change manager refocuses their attention.

The change manager works through the agenda and there are no issues with any of the requests for change. All are approved according to schedule. The implementation lead for the router firmware upgrade gives a brief update and explanation for the extension and this is nodded through. Finally, the change manager reports that the application change from Sunday has been successful and unless anyone has anything to raise now, it will be deployed to Southeast Asia and the USA the following weekend. All confirm that there have been no issues. The change manager will be ratifying go-ahead at the CAB summit on Wednesday but asks the assembled group to be vigilant and report anything untoward in the meantime.

After the meeting, the change manager tidies up the records and copies in any text compiled in the meeting, checking that approvals, status, implementation dates and so on reflect the current position. An updated summary is generated and made available in the group shared area. This snapshot represents a fixed record of what happened at the meeting and will be preserved for traceability. The change manager sends out a link to attendees, with copies to senior managers, and the change managers in Southeast Asia and the USA who will familiarise themselves with the content before the CAB summit tomorrow.

The change manager then generates a shorter summary status report, which will serve as a schedule of changes. This is made available to all staff on the change management intranet page and a message is pushed to everyone when it is available.

The local CAB meeting in Southeast Asia also took place at 10 a.m., local time, and the change manager there has already made the meeting record available. The UK change manager reads through it in preparation for the CAB summit tomorrow. The USA CAB meeting will take place later, but there will be enough time to read the outcomes in the morning.

One of the development team leads raises a request for approval on a new fast-track change based on a local deployment in the USA. Further checks confirm that it has been implemented successfully as a fast-track in the USA several times and CMS records indicate similar enough configuration and items affected. The change manager agrees in principle but will check for any issues in the USA at tomorrow's CAB summit and confirm a trial in the UK. The development team wants to go ahead next week and the request for change will need to be ready for the next CAB agenda.

Wednesday

The change manager has a brief update meeting with their line manager to report on yesterday's CAB meeting and take any input for the CAB summit. The meeting record is now in from yesterday's USA CAB, so it is time to review events over the pond.

The CAB summit takes place at noon GMT and is scheduled for an hour. Using technology for a virtual face-to-face meeting has improved communication. Video has made it much easier to anticipate transmission latency through visual cues and the meetings are smooth compared with earlier voice-only attempts. The change managers take turns to give a summary of their CAB outcome and share forthcoming plans. They discuss the cascade of the application update that was approved locally yesterday.

The UK change manager takes the opportunity to ask about the fast-track change that the UK development team wants to adopt, and the USA change manager confirms that it is well rehearsed and correlates closely to the UK environment. Obviously, they will need to review the impact and risk assessment in the context of that environment so it won't be an exact copy, but otherwise there should be no issues.

After the CAB summit, the UK change manager updates the development team lead who undertakes to review the impact and risk assessment on the fast-track request for local application. Once done, and peer reviewed, this will be submitted for ratification at the next local CAB meeting. The change manager flags it for the agenda, which will be prepared in draft form tomorrow, and schedules a review of the outcome with the development lead.

There is some time at the end of the day to do some compliance checks. As fast-track is a hot topic today, the change manager decides to spend an hour sampling fast-track requests for change and reviewing the outcomes to make sure that there have been no unforeseen impacts that should have required a reopening for full consideration and approval. It is usually easy enough to pick these up in real time because their status should be flagged appropriately through the CAB lifecycle, but it is possible to miss one from time to time if the status is incorrect.

Thursday

Closing in on the weekend again, it is time to check the status of changes approved at the CAB meeting and scheduled for implementation. Many will have been approved outright at the meeting, so no further action should be required, but some may have been given approval 'subject to' certain actions being complete. This is common, to avoid unnecessary delays to changes by deferring them to the next CAB meeting, and helps teams to make best use of their time.

The consequence, however, is that the change manager must represent the CAB and ensure that actions are complete, requests for change are updated and approvals are actioned in the system before changes can go ahead. The implementation teams know that they may not proceed on the strength of approval 'subject to' alone and must proactively seek explicit final approval from the change manager. However, in the heat of the moment it is easy to get carried away with the work at hand at the expense of the required documentation.

In the interests of keeping things moving, the change manager starts nudging for updates on Thursdays with a notional deadline of 2 p.m. on Fridays, after which they will lean heavily on the need for completion with the threat of rescinding approval. Rushing to finish at this stage can have negative consequences on the success of an implementation and the change manager is bound to act in the best interests of the business. It may be necessary to bring in product managers to discuss 'go' or 'no go' scenarios, and letting things go to the wire hampers that on a Friday afternoon.

At the same time, preparations for next week's CAB meeting are ramping up and the change manager will make available an early draft of the agenda for attendees to start considering. This will mean chasing up requests for change that are in the pipeline with looming tentative implementation dates. It is better to be proactive about this, and provide gentle reminders in advance of deadlines, than to let things drift into an argument later, which is not in the interests of the business and frankly is time wasting.

After generating the draft agenda for next week and pushing out a message to attendees that it is available, the change manager attends the monthly process and risk review meeting with R&D. Here, they will look at the fast-track change records that represent the changes applied in the last month and consider any issues or incidents that may have occurred as a result. On this occasion there has been a complaint from the R&D development team that their test environment server had been unexpectedly unavailable. This had caused them to delay a deployment, which had a knock-on effect in the business. It appeared that the cause was a communication issue. A new team of contractors had begun work in development and they had not been made aware that a change was due to be applied during a maintenance window, so they had planned to work late to meet a deadline and expected to be unhindered. The change manager undertook to talk to the procurement team to establish some points of contact for notification of new arrivals, so that communication plans could be updated accordingly.

Friday

Next week the reporting analyst will be compiling service level agreement (SLA) reports for the business, so the change manager needs to review records for the previous month to check that all are up to date with the correct status to reflect accurately in the reports. This also enables the change manager to reflect on successes and failures and provide some text for the reports analyst, who will add some context to the statistics for clarity. This is also a good time to check again that CMS records have been updated in case the configuration manager is preparing any reports that might be affected.

A meeting with a team initiating a new project is planned in order to discuss their overall approach and outline a timetable. The change manager will advise them on process requirements and help them to identify ways of incorporating what is needed into the request for change process at the appropriate times. The project team is familiar with the process, but it is helpful to look at the stages in the context of the critical path of new initiatives, and it is useful for the change manager to have them on the radar so they can be taken into account when considering other change plans. The project team has employed two new developers who start on Monday and the change manager has taken the opportunity to confirm an initial process induction requested by the service desk. Their rights to the change management system will be granted once this has been completed.

After that comes a final check of status on changes being implemented over the weekend and confirmation of approvals to go ahead on requests for change with 'subject to' outstanding actions, before signing off on the schedule with an update to all staff at 3 p.m.

The change manager reminds implementers that they should report any issues that occur as soon as possible and confirms their availability for calls at the weekend. This is especially important if there is going to be any impact on services on Monday morning, so that they can inform their line manager and the service desk manager, but it is also possible that overseas sites could be affected sooner, and the change manager can contact their opposite number in Southeast Asia and the USA to advise them. An early finish is swapped for the possibility of a few calls at the weekend, but hopefully no big issues.

THE DEVELOPING CHANGE MANAGER

The developing change manager is struggling with conflicting cultures and the difficulties associated with delivering a service in times of constraint but with the promise of more support in the future. Resources are stretched in order to cope with an increasing workload, making it difficult to manoeuvre sufficiently to improve the situation, but cooperation and collaboration can help to make breakthroughs.

Business and IT context

The developing change manager works for Company B, a specialist service provider in the UK that has been established for more than 20 years. It was recently bought by a Spanish company providing different but related services and is now wholly owned by them.

There are currently no plans to change the autonomy of Company B, which will continue to operate as a separate company, but a state of flux suggests more change to come and tensions in all departments are high. Company B was itself a merger of two companies and things have not really had the chance to settle fully before this new takeover. Consequently, there is a sense of frustration that utopia will never be reached.

Company B has consolidated the two merged companies into one building and has established one IT department over a period of time. Infrastructure management is split between a fileserver team and a networks team. These are undergoing a rationalisation on the one site and are made up of representatives of each company for continuity. There is a small development team that is struggling to manage a growing workload of service expansion requirements and plans to streamline business systems. Legacy applications on both sides are maintained by respective application support teams. There is a small consolidated service desk providing help for users in both companies and the staff are in the process of learning about each other's side of the business. Management acknowledge that the whole team is stretched, but it needs to see some evidence of the success of new products before it can make the case for investment in additional resources.

Background to change management

Company B and its new parent company have both implemented service management processes, including change management. Both companies have a change manager, but their processes and tools are quite different.

Process
Company B introduced change management after the merger with some success. There is a mixed culture in the new IT

department and attitude to change management varies. The fileserver team is mostly appreciative of the process and tends towards well-organised projects that comply with change management. The networks team has struggled with third-party maintenance providers inherited with the building, who have largely done their own thing. They are accustomed to being let on site without notice, often turning up unannounced, and the onsite IT team has become the dog that is wagged by the tail.

In the meantime, the development team is often under pressure to put changes into the live environment quickly, for 'live' testing, on irregular timescales. This is frequently at odds with the weekly change management and CAB meeting lifecycle that is in place. Furthermore, there is the maintenance of essential legacy systems that vies for priority to keep the business running normally day by day. The bureaucracy of change management is seen as too time-consuming when there is already so much else to do.

Tools

The tool in use is a change and configuration management system, but the configuration management part is largely empty apart from an array of configuration item types and attributes required. The consolidation of IT departments has brought fragmented records that are still managed locally by team. As changes have been made records haven't always been updated, but different expectations mean that planners don't know that what they are reading doesn't necessarily match what is out there. This means that the lengthy change management process is failing early without anyone realising it, because impact and risk assessments, and back-out plans, are based on inaccurate information. The system is not linked to the service desk system, so there is no direct correlation with incidents and problems.

Challenges facing the developing change manager

The core process has expanded to fill the time available without consideration of reporting and process improvement. There is a large volume of change coming from all areas, and it is as much as the change manager can do to tread water and keep the changes moving in line with business need. A week in the life of the developing change manager is invariably the same as the last.

Monday

The week starts with fallout from weekend changes that were under pressure to be approved but in the knowledge that configuration information was in short supply. There has been a tendency for changes, and even some back-outs, to go wrong, even though there has been a lengthy process of review and approval. The reality of the baseline all too often differs from what was written in the impact assessment, and changes are sometimes abandoned because the implementers simply weren't prepared and didn't have the right resources for the job that the change turned out to involve.

Most of the day can be taken up with post-implementation reviews, often in crisis mode, usually spontaneously as cause and effect become known. Dissemination can be chaotic because line management allegiances may take precedence over change management process requirements. This means that the change manager could even be the last to know when something goes wrong. Add to that the continual nature of change planning and the constant stream of new requirements and requests for help with the process, and it is easy to see how the change manager is in reactive mode at all times, unable to take control from the top down.

Tuesday

Tuesday starts the ramp up to the CAB meeting on Wednesday. The agenda must be prepared and circulated to attendees and this can be time-consuming. It is prepared in a spreadsheet and is based on the previous week's meeting record, rolling forward outstanding changes still in the planning stage and up for discussion.

The agenda is meant to be sent out around midday on Tuesday, to allow plenty of time for review in advance of the meeting, but it is often delayed into the afternoon. Implementation teams know the deadline for inclusion on the agenda and there are often last-minute requests to include new changes that haven't been fully written. The nature of the workload is such that business and IT managers often overrule the process to push things through in order to satisfy business pressure. Risks become riskier when experience shows what can happen on a Monday morning, but risks must be taken.

The change manager finds themself chasing completion of the agenda, only to have to reissue it with a late amendment anyway.

Wednesday
The CAB meeting takes place on Wednesday and it is sometimes standing room only. The change manager runs the meeting using a print-out of the agenda and makes handwritten notes on decisions, which is quicker than trying to type them into the spreadsheet in real time. This makes the meeting length as manageable as possible and enables the change manager to focus on controlling what can sometimes be a heated discussion, but the trade-off is rework after the meeting to prepare the notes.

The meeting can be chaotic, partly because of the number of attendees required to explain their last-minute plans and partly because the agenda was issued too late for people to adequately prepare. Because of the late nature of many of the requests for change, they are more likely to be approved 'subject to' further action between the meeting and the implementation, which is not necessarily confined to the weekend. This will mean more chasing up to complete approvals in the second half of the week.

Almost always the rest of the day is taken up with more queries and late changes still trying to squeeze in for approval, as well as new requests getting in early for next week. The meeting record is completed eventually, after many interruptions, and is sent out to attendees by email. This is also the schedule of change and, importantly, actions for those still completing requirements for final sign off.

Thursday

Thursday is more of the same. Chasing implementation teams for updates on their approved 'subject to' actions; fielding requests for help; and getting new plans into the process. Overnight changes might be scheduled in advance of the weekend and on any day the networks team could announce the arrival of a supplier wanting to apply seemingly spontaneous changes. Although these might be routine as far as the supplier is concerned, there is no process in place to require them to provide notice and the change manager must make the call between classifying the change as an emergency, with a cursory glance at the impact, or causing unnecessary expense by rescheduling.

Friday

By Friday the change manager is experiencing regular conflicts over application changes that must go in over the weekend but which missed the CAB meeting on Wednesday. The change manager is reluctant to invoke the emergency process every time this happens – because they are not emergencies and it could open the floodgates to abuse of the process – but they acknowledge that there is a timing mismatch.

Unfortunately, it is difficult to reschedule the CAB because it already aligns with other requirements and the current timing suits the people who attend. The change manager's line manager has agreed to help by convening a pseudo-CAB meeting with their peers and business representatives on Friday mornings to maintain the process without the overheads associated with the emergency change process. This is effectively the emergency change process invoked predictably every week, to ensure that approvers are available to push things through. It also frees up the change manager to deal with real emergencies and get home at a decent time on a Friday.

The change manager might get a call over the weekend with an update on changes scheduled, but that's preferable to finding out on Monday morning (or being the last to know), especially if something has failed or been backed-out. They can advise the service desk manager to put a couple of extra bodies on the early shift too, which the implementation teams and their managers don't usually consider. More often than not, though, escalation of failed changes rises through the implementation teams' line management and a peaceful weekend comes to an abrupt close on Monday.

Opportunities for improvement

At face value it looks as though the process is just a vehicle for advertising widely the failures of IT. There is also a creeping sense that senior management are becoming increasingly frustrated with the perceived obstruction of change by the change management process. But without it, there is no traceability of change and even though failures are high profile when they happen, their visibility is a good thing for improvement, even if it is not such good PR for the IT department.

As it is, due to the sheer volume of change in the present circumstances, actual change has a rhythm of its own outside the change management process, which is trying to get noticed but is often perceived to be just in the way. The change manager is always playing catch-up and is left with little or no time to consider process improvement.

The change manager knows that reporting is the key to raising awareness of the process's value and is starting to identify opportunities for improvement. They are trying to establish some basic reporting, to understand the bottlenecks better but also track what feels like an increasing volume of change, so that they can begin to make the case for help if the trend continues. One of the service desk analysts is interested in reporting and the change manager has gratefully accepted the offer of help.

There are currently no fast-track changes to help speed things up and take the load off, partly because the change manager hasn't the time to address them, and partly because the success rate for change is so low it seems unlikely that any could be promoted to fast-track. This is an area to be developed and the change manager plans to sit down with the networks team and their telecoms supplier to flesh out some standard approaches. Combined with a schedule from the supplier, this should be a quick win that will start to chip away at the disruption caused by unplanned work.

In the meantime, news has just come through that the parent company has now announced that it wants to consolidate infrastructure architecture and suppliers so that Company B is aligned with them. Although this had not initially been expected, the parent company has found it can make significant cost savings by streamlining providers.

The good news is that the parent company will provide the resources to project manage and implement the changes; the bad news is that it means more changes through the UK change management process, which must be made available to the Spanish team. However, this will also be an opportunity to understand each other's processes better, which will be necessary since the ground-rules are quite different.

The parent company has a heavy emphasis on standardised changes with automatic approvals, built into service level agreements. They have a monthly CAB meeting for non-standard changes, which are treated as exceptions to the norm. Often the emergency process is used between CAB meetings to meet project deadlines, but not because they are emergencies. The change manager in the parent company is also the IT operations manager and doesn't want to increase the frequency of CAB meetings, which will take up more time, but they must balance this with the disruption caused by invoking the emergency change process. It is not an ideal situation, but the rapid growth of the company has stretched everyone. The Spanish team will need to fully appreciate that fast-tracking everything is not going to work in the UK climate, but the UK change manager can learn first-hand how well fast-track can work. There are good and bad points for both sides and there is an opportunity to learn from each other.

Furthermore, the Spanish company wants to consolidate IT service management tools and will update the UK team's resources with their integrated system. This will help the change manager jump-start the reports development and bring them in line with the latest tools. The Spanish change manager will work with the UK change manager on the configuration, but the UK change manager is expected to contribute their own configuration needs to enable the best solution for Company B's primary operation. The UK change manager has learned a lot about how well the process does and doesn't work, without the reports, by having been so immersed in change, and is in a good position to leap up to the next level. Better still, their line manager has agreed to fund some language classes for personal development and they will spend a week in the Spanish office looking at how they do things there. There is even talk of the change managers providing cover for each other in the future when things are more settled.

THE GETTING STARTED CHANGE MANAGER

The getting started change manager faces the paradox of introducing more effort to reduce existing overload, with a blank page and no tools. Justifying the time and effort required can be difficult, but small steps can demonstrate value and encouragement and begin the path to continual improvement.

Business and IT background

The getting started change manager works for Company C, a not-for-profit company in the UK education sector. It has a small IT team supporting a single site in Manchester. Service desk duties are shared around four analysts, who combine this with other work including technical implementation and maintenance of the infrastructure. A hands-on IT manager is responsible for maintaining capacity, hardware and operating systems, as well as the network, and oversees the work of the others.

There is a web development team introducing a new content management system and streamlining many small applications into one system. There is also a lot of distributed documentation, electronic and paper, and there is a project to introduce a company-wide document management system.

These initiatives are driven by a major organisational change programme. The company has grown organically from the bottom up. Departments have funded and introduced their own applications, and some infrastructure such as PCs and printers. Over time, this has been networked and an evolving central IT department has attempted to manage disparate systems. The amount of physical paperwork has long outgrown the building, which is in prime space. The aim is to reduce the footprint of the company by getting rid of as much of the paper as possible and moving into smaller, cheaper accommodation. All departments, including IT, are under pressure to reduce headcount.

As personnel turnover has refreshed over the years, assumptions about the roles and responsibilities of the IT team have evolved. Originally, as departments bought their own equipment, they were responsible for supporting it themselves, because in the beginning there was no IT department. Now, as the concept of calling a service desk has become more familiar, joiners to the company assume that they can get support from the IT team. Undeterred by the lack of a service desk telephone number, even un-intrepid seekers of help can locate them easily in the middle of the large open plan office, bounded on all sides by operational teams.

The rotational service desk is thus a notional concept, borne out of the reality of the situation but cobbled together in an attempt to protect at least some of the team from interruption. In principle they welcome the extra work as it should protect them from job losses, but they are coming under increasing pressure to fix systems that they know nothing about. This is having an impact on their ability to handle the throughput of change coming from the two projects, both of which have a high profile in the strategic aims of the company. Demands for implementation from each project frequently arrive unannounced, often together, and invariably requiring urgent attention. The IT team are under pressure from all sides and priority comes down to who shouts the loudest or who is standing over them.

Background to change management

There is no change management at present.

Introducing the process

The IT manager thinks that change management could help, but is understandably wary of introducing a whole new process in the middle of a restructure for dwindling staff numbers to take part in. Also, the learning curve for all involved could be too much in an already stretched environment. Hiring a change manager is not an option, so the IT manager has to run things and, knowing how old habits die hard, they are concerned about the amount of work involved in monitoring compliance. All that without considering that it will almost certainly slow down the projects and could make the department look like it is blocking progress on the main aims of the organisation.

Given the natural scale of things, then, the IT manager has decided to do something but start small. Change management workflow tools do not exist in the organisation; there is now a very basic system for logging support calls – to attempt to track and quantify the work being done – and an asset management module that is not used, but nothing else. Money will not be forthcoming to buy something, and anyway they don't really know what they are doing yet and wouldn't know where to begin to buy something that they would then need to configure and learn how to use.

In the meantime, an internet search produced a checklist of contents for a request for change, which was used to create a basic document template using generic productivity tools already available. It seemed that starting just with the projects could limit the initial workload and could be positioned as helping to meet deadlines, given the generally chaotic nature of the support team's priorities.

The IT manager sat down with the two project managers to discuss the proposal and explained that the IT team needed to know what was coming through so they could plan their work. It wasn't just a case of reacting to demand, they needed to make sure that they understood the impact of the work on other services so they could protect them or arrange downtime with the business. The IT manager could help them, too, by providing configuration information from their own baseline records stored in spreadsheets, which would help them with their planning as well as the impact and risk assessments. The project managers agreed to fill in the templates with input from the IT manager and update them as plans developed. The IT manager could use them to build a schedule and a plan for implementation and could use the impact assessment information to talk to the right service users to warn them of potential disruption (there are no service level agreements and no other customer interfaces with IT). Furthermore, the information provided in the requests for change could be used to update the IT manager's configuration spreadsheets, ensuring continuity and quality assurance.

Monitoring impact
Keen to monitor the impact of the initiative, the IT manager decided to create a new category in the service desk tool to identify changes rather than incidents. The IT manager created a record for each change with basic data as a master record. Over time, as the number of documents increased, they could be filtered into a separate list. Although only an onscreen filter, it will make it easier to capture the data in a spreadsheet and produce some crude reporting, to show volume of work and allow the IT manager to reflect on the evolving process. In this way they will be able to convey what has been achieved with minimal impact on workload at no additional cost, and this could help them to develop a business case for implementing a full process. Trying it out on paper also made adjustments relatively easy, with

an opportunity for some lessons to be learned before implementing an expensive configuration.

Most importantly, the IT team now has sight of a schedule, so they can effectively prioritise their work. There are fewer complaints from users who are not able to access systems they didn't know were unavailable, because the IT manager is able to communicate this to them in advance. Users are still not always happy about it but being informed is a step in the right direction. The experiment has demonstrated that with a small change, it is possible to get a handle on improving how things are done, however busy the IT team are. Without doing something, they were doomed forever to fire-fight with an ever-decreasing reputation. A small intervention was all it took to take back control, stop reacting and start directing. As the emerging face of IT for the end-users, this is essential for their credibility in customer service.

The role going forwards

The reorganisation is still ongoing, but the efforts of the IT team, in cooperation with the two projects, has not gone unnoticed. The success of the trial request for change document has led to the template being used for other changes being planned within IT, such as infrastructure maintenance and server upgrades, and this has improved the success rate.

One notable benefit came from thinking through in advance the requirements for backing-out an operating system upgrade and including details of the media registration codes in the request for change. This proved fortuitous when the change did need to be backed-out on the day and having the codes ready meant the difference between comfortably restoring service and scrambling to prevent an outage, not knowing where the codes were. What could have been a hectic and apologetic Monday morning was just as if nothing had happened for the end-users. Well nothing material had! However, the IT team learned a lot and for them it was a success of sorts, so the IT manager made a point of it at the weekly management meeting.

As a result, senior managers are becoming more aware of the unseen aspects of delivering good service and are now convinced of the need for better organisation and process in the IT team, as their profile increases in the user base. Since they have committed to maintaining in-house content and document management systems, they now realise that it must be worth investing in the processes to support them properly as well. They are planning to upgrade the service desk tool to incorporate change management and the IT manager is booked onto a service management foundation course to learn more about what they need to do going forward.

The change manager 'hat'

The IT manager is still the IT manager in name, but now wears the change manager role 'hat' as well. Time and resources are still tight, so the role must be absorbed into other commitments.

The weekly management meeting has all the appropriate representation required for a CAB, so there is now a standing agenda item to discuss forthcoming change at the end of that meeting. The IT manager dons the change manager 'hat' to facilitate that part of the discussion and, afterwards, to produce a schedule of change and a communication plan for the business.

While the CAB meeting has been absorbed reasonably efficiently, the role is expanding in terms of providing guidance for the completion of new requests for change. However, this is preferable to the old ways of working because advance information can be shared with the rest of the support team and the team's work schedule can be plotted early. The time spent proactively in planning sessions with project and other managers is much more manageable than the time spent reacting to conflicting priorities and disrupted effort.

The IT manager is updating their configuration spreadsheets with the outputs from the requests for change, as this requires the least effort for the greatest return. However, they have committed to look at the asset management part of the call logging system for ideas on integrated configuration management going forwards (but that's another 'hat'!).

Continual improvement

The success of the intervention has been the result of starting small and winning over one or two people, rather than trying to change the world overnight and meeting too much resistance. Approaching the project managers with an offer of mutual support showed openness to the needs and perspectives of others and a willingness to help rather than hinder the business changes, which, after all, are in the interests of the whole organisation, including the IT department.

There is still a long way to go to automate a change management process, but the journey has begun. One of the project managers has been assigned to lead the selection and implementation of the new service management system and the IT manager is a key stakeholder who will contribute process and reporting requirements for its configuration. The involvement of the project manager means that the IT manager can continue to focus primarily on the operational aspects of the role while the plan is developed for the process design, tool selection and configuration, administrator and user training, and so on. Including other stakeholders from the start will also ensure the best chance of success for implementation and compliance, because the process will be designed with their needs in mind.

For the time being, the role of change manager is manageable for the IT manager alongside existing responsibilities. Whether or not a full-time change manager will be needed remains to be seen. Once the business transformation projects are complete, the amount of change throughput might decrease significantly. On the other hand, the efficient processing of change could reduce the negative impact on the IT team, allowing someone to step up to the role. Either way, time is better spent on proactive measures.

KEY POINTS

- The change manager role can exist at different levels of maturity, anywhere on a continuum between all and nothing.

- Cooperation and collaboration are essential to make the change management process work and ensure that the change manager role can fulfil its potential.

- Constant fire-fighting does not preclude process improvement. Quick wins and small-scale interventions provide the leverage for continual improvement, which is the only course of action to break a vicious cycle.

APPENDIX: REFERENCES AND FURTHER READING

All sources cited in earlier chapters are referenced in footnotes as they appear. References to relevant topics previously discussed are included in this section for completeness alongside other ideas for further reading around the role of change manager.

ACCESSIBILITY

Accessibility for all is important to recognise when designing systems and processes. The Web Content Accessibility Guidelines (WCAG) describe good practice for making websites, applications and other digital creations more accessible and usable for everyone. More information can be found here: www.w3.org/WAI/standards-guidelines/wcag/. Also, BCS has a Digital Accessibility Specialist Group that promises to 'provide tools and techniques to inform IT professionals on DA best practice', amongst other things. Full details about the group can be found on the BCS website at: www.bcs.org/category/18035.

In the UK, diversity is protected by law in the Equality Act 2010, details of which can be found here: www.legislation.gov.uk/ukpga/2010/15/contents. The Human Rights Commission provides further guidance at: www.equalityhumanrights.com/en/equality-act-2010/what-equality-act.

AGILE

Agile methods of software development are arguably more common now than more traditional waterfall approaches, making the need for Agile change management critical to success. For more information about Agile methods see the Manifesto for Agile Software Development at: http://agilemanifesto.org/. The Scrum Alliance outlines one such Agile method at: www.scrumalliance.org/. DevOps is another, with information to be found at: https://itrevolution.com/

It is worth bearing in mind that as approaches such as these become mainstream and concepts are adopted and adapted, they become distorted from the intentions of their originator and so the terms become generic. There are also wider applications of the Agile concept, for example in PRINCE2 Agile®[1] and generic product development such as The Lean Startup.[2]

BCS BOOKS

BCS Bookshop is an online store for BCS published business and IT books. Titles referred to explicitly in this book are *Business Writing for Technical People* and *Technical Writing for Business People*. To see the full range of titles, go to: http://shop.bcs.org/.

The BCS Guides to IT Roles series covers a range of IT roles, some explicitly mentioned in this book as connected with the change manager; for example, *Problem Manager* and *Service Level Manager*.

CHANGE MANAGEMENT (ORGANISATIONAL)

Change management in the wider context of organisational change is a huge related topic, and a good place to start looking into this is the Change Management Institute (CMI)

---

1 www.axelos.com/best-practice-solutions/prince2-agile

2 http://theleanstartup.com/

at: www.change-management-institute.com/ and its Change Management Body of Knowledge and other capability tools and opportunities.

FRAMEWORKS

Best practice, or good practice, frameworks containing technical change management include ITIL® and COBIT®. For further information about ITIL®, go to the Axelos website at: www.axelos.com/best-practice-solutions/itil. Details on COBIT® from ISACA are at: www.isaca.org/cobit/pages/default.aspx. The ITIL® suite of publications is published by The Stationery Office. ITIL® Practitioner Guidance provides useful approaches to implementation. Full details of all the ITIL® books are available on The Stationery Office website at: www.tsoshop.co.uk/AXELOS-Global-Best-Practice/ITIL/.

LEGISLATION

The National Archives publishes all UK legislation at www.legislation.gov.uk. Legislation that applies generically in any context includes the Data Protection Act 2018, the Equality Act 2010, the Computer Misuse Act 1990 and the Health and Safety at Work Act 1974, and changes might feasibly be required for legal compliance.

MEMBERSHIP BODIES

Membership organisations relating to technical change management include BCS and itSMF. BCS is The Chartered Institute for IT and is a membership organisation for those in related fields. For more information on BCS membership services and benefits, visit the BCS website at: www.bcs.org. The itSMF represents IT service management professionals in the UK: www.itsmf.co.uk/ and internationally: www.itsmfi.org/.

PROJECT MANAGEMENT

Project management methods are many and varied. Notably Axelos is responsible for PRINCE2®: www.axelos.com/best-practice-solutions/prince2 and PRINCE2 Agile®: www.axelos.com/best-practice-solutions/prince2-agile.

The W. Edwards Deming Institute perpetuates the legacy of The Deming System of Profound Knowledge®, which represents a holistic approach to leadership and management. For full details go to: https://deming.org/.

QUALIFICATIONS AND CERTIFICATIONS

Qualifications and certifications relating to change management are available. For example, BCS provides the BCS Specialist Certificate in Change Management. More details can be found here: https://certifications.bcs.org/category/15480. ITIL® is another common source of related qualifications. For up-to-date options go to: www.axelos.com/certifications/itil-certifications.

T Levels are two-year, technical programmes designed with employers to give young people the skills that industry needs. From 2020, they will give students aged 16 to 18 a technical alternative to A levels and will help them to get a skilled job. T Levels will offer students a mixture of classroom- or workshop-based learning and 'on-the-job' experience in industries including digital subject areas. More information about T levels can be found at: www.gov.uk/government/publications/introduction-of-t-levels. See also the Institute of Apprenticeships at: www.instituteforapprenticeships.org/.

QUALITY MANAGEMENT

The Chartered Quality Institute (CQI) is a global professional body advancing the practice of quality management in all sectors. For more information go to: www.quality.org/.

SFIA AND SFIA*PLUS*

SFIA is the Skills Framework for the Information Age, providing a common language for skills in the digital world. The SFIA Foundation maintains the SFIA Framework, which is used widely throughout the world for skills and competency development. The SFIA Framework is readily available, in 10 languages, from the SFIA website at: www.sfia-online.org and while there is a modest licence fee for commercial exploitation, the vast majority of use is free of charge.

SFIA**plus** is a development of SFIA produced by BCS for its members. It provides career development guidance on all the skills in the SFIA Framework, describing typical work activities, knowledge, skills and behaviours expected, appropriate training options, personal development activities and qualifications. More information on this and other BCS membership services and benefits can be found on the BCS website at: www.bcs.org.

STANDARDS

Standards mentioned in this book are limited to ISO/IEC 20000, ISO 9001 and ISO 44001, but there are many standards ranging across the industry. For more information, see the International Organization for Standardization website at: www.iso.org/home.html and the British Standards Institution website at: www.bsigroup.com.

TOOLS

Locating up-to-date information about specific tools to support the change manager is best left to a search engine, since there are so many and they are so liable to change. Commercially developed tools typically come at a cost for a variety of licensing and deployment models. Open source tools are also available. These are typically free to use and adapt, but support may be limited. Some offer commercial support contracts; others no more than an online community of other users. If you intend to rely on community support check that it is active before you take the plunge, or you could struggle to get help. For more information about open source, go to: https://opensource.org/.

INDEX